PHILADELPHIA'S

Strawbridge &Clothier

PHILADELPHIA'S

Strawbridge & Clothier

• From Our Family to Yours •

MARGARET STRAWBRIDGE BUTTERWORTH

THE
History
PRESS

Published by The History Press
Charleston, SC
www.historypress.com

First published 2023

Manufactured in the United States

ISBN 9781467150262

Library of Congress Control Number: 2022950063

Notice: The information in this book is true and complete to the best of our knowledge. It is offered without guarantee on the part of the author or The History Press. The author and The History Press disclaim all liability in connection with the use of this book.

Top: S&C logo. *Middle*: Clover logo. *Bottom*: Seal of Confidence. *Courtesy of the author.*

Dedicated to Elizabeth Ann Strawbridge Nord, "Aunt Nancy"—the best aunt anyone could have. You obliged my never-ending childish pleas to tell me stories about "when you were a kid" growing up in our family. You jokingly told me I had enough stories to write a book. Although I haven't written a book about our family (yet), here's one about the Store Family.

CONTENTS

Contents

ACKNOWLEDGEMENTS

I owe a sincere thank-you to the following:

Former S&C and Clover employees who made time for me, answered my Facebook posts and direct inquiries and provided me with stories, photos and memorabilia of their time with the company.

Members of the Strawbridge and Clothier families who agreed to the writing of this book, supported me in my research and shared their own stories with me.

The Hagley Museum and Library's enormous collection of Strawbridge & Clothier archives, with particular thanks to reference archivist and digital archives specialist Angela Schad, who responded to my numerous requests for high-resolution scans of images.

Alfred Lief, the author of *Family Business: A Century in the Life and Times of Strawbridge & Clothier*.

Frank Veale, whom I wish were alive today to thank in person for his tremendous recounting of S&C during the 1970s and 1980s in his books *Family Business: Strawbridge & Clothier: The Momentous Seventies* and *Family Business: Strawbridge & Clothier: The Triumphant Eighties*.

Steven L. Strawbridge, whose book *Family Business: Strawbridge & Clothier: The Final Years* was an invaluable resource.

The Historical Society of Pennsylvania.

The Philadelphia Inquirer Archives.

The GIANT Company, with special thanks to Ashley Flower.

Jennifer Slobotkin of SobycoPR.

The following dear friends who were supportive cheerleaders: Rachel Acosta, Leslie Curran, Shawne Johnson, my AIS crew, Barbara Luetke, Ronit Plank, the SPARRC Team, Missy Ponder Reston and Birgit Walbaum.

Finally, Bob, Gavin and Mackenna, this book could have never happened without your support and love.

INTRODUCTION

In July 1996, I helped my father pack up what few belongings he had left in his tenth-floor office of the Eighth and Market Streets Strawbridge & Clothier store. It was the summer before my senior year of college. I had taken time off from my summer job to help him. Twenty-six years later, my memory of that day is not as vivid as it once was. What does stand out to me, though, is how empty his office felt. It once held a large, dark wooden desk; a formal but comfortable couch, chairs and a coffee table; several family photos, pleasantly framed and displayed; and a large oil painting of my great-grandfather Francis Reeves Strawbridge, my father's namesake. There was one window in the room, a tall, wide window that looked down onto the hustle and bustle of Market Street and filled the spacious room with plenty of sunlight. It had a deep windowsill where my father kept a couple of potted plants, one of which was a cactus. What kind of cactus? I don't know. I just recall that out of the terra-cotta pot grew a small, green, spiky stalk.

We had a dolly to load my father's belongings on and wheel out of the office. We placed the cactus there, along with some books and file boxes. As we wheeled the dolly carefully out of the room and made our way down "mahogany row" (which was the nickname for the row of offices that housed the company's officers) out toward the tenth-floor lobby and to the freight elevator, my father kept a pleasant smile on his face. We passed by several other employees who were also packing up their last few belongings, many of whom approached my father, each taking a turn to wish the other well in their future endeavors. As I kept a steady hand on the potted cactus, making sure it wouldn't tip off the dolly, I snuck glances at him, trying to detect any sign of sadness, perhaps a stray tear escaping from the corner of his eye. This would be the last time he would pass through the halls and floors of the grand, thirteen-story limestone building where he worked six days a week for thirty-five years. It was where he visited his father and grandfather in their tenth-floor offices as a child, where he and his family shopped, where he took business lunches in the stately sixth-floor Corinthian Dining Room, where he made daily rounds on the shopping floor greeting sales staff and fellow "Associates," as all Strawbridge & Clothier (and Clover) employees were called. He was not just saying goodbye to a space; he was saying goodbye to a life. Not surprisingly, there were no tears, no visible sign of melancholy. What could I expect from a man who was so deeply a product of his generation and a family that didn't wear their emotions on their sleeves?

What my twenty-one-year-old self couldn't see was that he was keeping it together. The emotions were there, they were real, but he was simply doing what he had always had to do in his career as a member of the fourth and last generation to manage and run the family business. He had to keep it together. Even when things were falling apart.

When we got back to our house, the potted cactus found a new home in our sunroom, where my mother lovingly nursed a variety of houseplants. My father slowly adjusted to his life of retirement. Years later, as a young adult trying to make her own way through life on the other side of the country, I would return to my childhood home to visit my parents. I would sit with my father in the sunroom and talk. From time to time, I would notice the cactus and remark on how much it had grown, the stalk now nearly two feet high with a few newly formed arms. It had kept itself together.

From 1868 to 1996, Strawbridge & Clothier, whose flagship store was located on Eighth and Market Streets in the heart of Philadelphia, strove to meet the needs of its customers. First serving the "Quaker City," the department store later branched out to nearby New Jersey and Delaware in the mid- to late twentieth century and developed a discount division called Clover. Built on the "foundation stones of integrity and character," S&C and its founders, Justus C. Strawbridge and Isaac H. Clothier, two Pennsylvania Quakers, stood out among most merchants of the time. The two Friends aspired to establish a culture of consumer confidence, quality and friendly service. The customer was always right; the price was always just. At the time of its sale in 1996 to the May Department Stores Company (now Macy's, Inc.) S&C was the oldest department store in the country with continuous family involvement in the management and ownership of the company. This leadership spread over four generations, with a fifth beginning to emerge in its final years.

The story of Strawbridge & Clothier goes beyond its founders and their descendants, however. The employees made the store what it was. They were part of a shared experience that shaped their professional and personal lives. For two years, I have spoken with numerous past employees of both Strawbridge & Clothier and Clover. Each graciously shared their memories of their time with the company. Our conversations were filled with laughter, heartfelt sentiment and bittersweet tears. Growing up a Strawbridge, I was always aware of my family's name recognition in the region. Yet youth can be ignorant. I didn't fully appreciate what exactly went into making sure the doors of each branch store opened every day to thousands of customers and then closed in the evening, only to prepare for the next day: the physical labor, organization, planning, analysis and constant risk assessment, all to keep the customer happy and returning. Perhaps more important, though, was to keep the employees happy and returning. Thanks to the openness of everyone I spoke with, I have learned to more deeply appreciate how they kept the machine running.

This book is my attempt to tell the history of Strawbridge & Clothier, once one of the Delaware Valley's largest employers, and to bring that history alive through a selection of employee memories. Through this unique perspective, we learn how a "Store Family" was created and how its 128-year existence was deeply woven into the history of the region.

It was one family....The company cared for its people. It was the last employer that still subscribed to that employee-employer contract. If you work hard for the company, the company will be good to you.
—*Pete O'Grady, Clover division Associate*

CHAPTER 1

A STORE IS BORN

But the man who has acquired wealth and has not acquired the respect of his fellow men, and especially of his own people—those who have aided in building his fortune—is not a successful man.
—Isaac H. Clothier

A person could fulfill all their shopping needs while strolling along Philadelphia's wide and expansive Market Street in the 1860s. Groceries, china, furniture, glassware, hardware and more could be found in the shops and market stands lining either side of the street. Cutting through the City of Brotherly Love's center, Market Street was and remains today one of Philadelphia's primary east–west thoroughfares. Nineteenth-century pedestrians walked carefully on sidewalks along the cobblestone streets, staying clear of the trolley tracks laid by the Pennsylvania Railroad extending down to Dock Street Market, a large wholesale produce market. Freight cars drawn by mules led by a bell mare rode the tracks. The occasional crack of long, black whips held by blue-shirted drivers filled the air.[1] Farmers and butchers sold their produce from sheds that stood in the middle of Market Street just east of Eighth Street. A lively scene, perhaps, but Market Street would become ever more bustling in the coming decades.

To meet their dry goods needs (fabrics, threads and clothing, as opposed to groceries and hardware), a shopper would arrive at the northwest corner of Eighth and Market Streets. Here stood a small, colonial-era, three-story red brick building that, a century earlier, had been the office of the Department of State, where Thomas Jefferson performed his duties as secretary of state.

J.C. Strawbridge & Co. store at Eighth and Market Streets, 1862. *Courtesy of the Hagley Museum and Library.*

Approximately twenty-four by twenty-four feet, the building now held a variety of fabrics to purchase for clothes making. Although men's clothes were beginning to be made in factories, there were not many options for women to buy ready-made dresses. For them, clothes making was primarily done at home on their sewing machines or by one of the numerous dressmakers in the city, for those who could afford it. Also on display in the tiny shop were blankets, tablecloths and napkins, towels, chintzes for curtain making and other household needs. Merchandise was on the ground floor only. According to business historian Alfred Lief in his book *Family Business*, shoppers didn't like to climb stairs at the time.[2]

The store was called J.C. Strawbridge & Co., and the young co-owner was Justus Clayton Strawbridge. Having started his career in retail at the age of fifteen as a clerk for a small dry goods store, Justus had gained enough confidence and experience by the age of twenty-three to enter a partnership with fellow retailer Joseph Cowperthwait Jr. On June 1, 1861, the two signed an agreement and opened the centrally located store on Market Street. By 1864, Cowperthwait had left the partnership; he was briefly replaced by a Lewis Weaver. In 1868, Justus was yet again in search of a replacement after Weaver's departure.

Enter Isaac H. Clothier, an honest wholesale cloth dealer who had developed a friendship with Justus over the past few years while selling his wares to the store. He seemed the perfect candidate to Justus. In addition to their common interest in retail, the two men were less than a year apart in age and shared a deep Quaker faith, which would instruct their business practices.

Founded as the Religious Society of Friends by George Fox in the mid-1600s in England, the Quaker religion exercises the principles of justice, equality and peace. Early Quakers believed that the "Spirit" or "Inner Light" rests in each person and provides direct access to God without the need for a preacher or intermediary. Members would tremble as they sat in silent worship together waiting for the voice of God to move them to speak. Hence the nickname "Quakers," which was originally intended to ridicule members but instead was adopted by them. Pennsylvania was founded as a Quaker colony in 1681 by William Penn. Today, there are fewer than fifteen thousand Quakers in Philadelphia and more than three hundred thousand around the world.[*]

---

* Emma J. Lapsansky Werner, "Quaker City," The Encyclopedia of Greater Philadelphia, accessed August 31, 2022, https://philadelphiaencyclopedia.org/themes/quaker-city/; FJ Staff, "New Worldwide Quaker Map Released," Friends Journal, September 13, 2017, https://www.friendsjournal.org/new-worldwide-quaker-released/.

On July 1, 1868, at the age of thirty, the two Friends joined in partnership to form Strawbridge & Clothier at 801–803 Market Street. This was the site of Justus's charming little dry goods store, which he and Isaac had replaced with a newly erected five-story building, forty-two feet on Market and sixty-seven feet on Eighth. The first floor and basement were the sales floors, the second floor was rented out to other businesses and the top floors were reserved for storing stock.[3] Justus and Isaac shared a large flattop desk in a corner in the basement, but as one of the store's early employees recalled, the two chairs were seldom occupied, "as the Firm were busy elsewhere."[4] In addition to running the store, the partners were often away doing most of the merchandise buying. Justus bought silks and dress goods; Isaac bought the cloth for men's clothing. Bob Dillon, who assisted Justus and Isaac, bought shawls.

Quaker merchants like Justus and Isaac distinguished themselves by bringing integrity and honesty to business, standards that were difficult to come by in the nineteenth century when shopkeepers did not commonly display the price of goods. Purchases were typically done through price haggling, creating an atmosphere of distrust between seller and buyer. It wasn't until Alexander Turney Stewart, the "father of the American Department store," opened his dry goods store in New York in 1823, that the concept of "no haggle" shopping

Top: Justus C. Strawbridge. *Bottom*: Isaac H. Clothier. *Courtesy of the Hagley Museum and Library.*

was introduced.[5] Although the concept was still catching on in the 1860s, it appealed to several retailers, like Justus and Isaac, whose religious convictions, specifically around equality, deeply influenced their business operations.

S&C's early advertisements touted the quality of goods sold at only one price and publicized the store's policy to purchase and sell only for cash. A retail world without credit purchases might seem unfathomable to today's consumer, but Justus and Isaac shunned credit, believing that relying on it would cheat the customer: "the paying customer is not therefore taxed to help pay the debt of a customer who does not pay."[6]

Equally as important to the two men was customer service. They assured customers that "correctness of representation and the utmost politeness" was required of their employees.[7] According to Isaac H. Clothier,

The Undersigned desire to inform you that they have formed a CO-PARTNERSHIP under the firm name of

STRAWBRIDGE & CLOTHIER,

for the transaction of the

RETAIL AND WHOLESALE

General Dry Goods Business,

in their New Building, just erected, at the corner of Eighth and Market Streets.

J. C. STRAWBRIDGE,
ISAAC H. CLOTHIER.

Philadelphia, 9th mo. 1st, 1868.

Announcement of partnership from a circular sent to a mailing list. *Courtesy of the Hagley Museum and Library.*

The idea in our minds, when we started as young men was to build our business on the foundation stones of integrity and character. We greatly desired to acquire fortune, but that was not the sole and primal idea, for we believed that if we acquired fortune only, our lives would not be successful in the highest sense. As one of the steps to a broad and generous success, we strove from the first to draw near to our people and draw them near to us.

There was great potential to acquire fortune in 1868. Philadelphia was home to more than five hundred thousand residents. It had survived the war thanks to its textile mills, which readily supplied wool to the military. The economy continued to boom in peacetime, giving people more disposable income. Market Street became even more vital to the city, as more trolley lines were established by the Pennsylvania Railroad and the street became a governmental and commercial hub.[8] By 1871, plans to erect a new city hall were underway at the intersection of Market and Broad Streets in the center of downtown. By 1880, Philadelphia was the second-largest city in the United States.

Attitudes changed over time. After World War I, credit was commonly accepted in retail, and by 1919, S&C had created a deferred payment accounts division.[*]

_____

[*] Lief, *Family Business*, 148.

Given this environment, it didn't take long for Justus and Isaac to see returns on their investment. In its first thirty years, the store would expand its location four times, eventually taking up more than half a city block. Merchandise was no longer limited to fabrics for women's clothing and household linens but had expanded into men's and children's clothing, shoes, accessories, furs, upholstery, carpets, books, candy and even bicycles. Its customer base spread from the city into the growing suburbs, and the number of employees swelled one-hundredfold. The competition grew, too. John Wanamaker opened his clothing store in 1861 at Sixth and Market and, in 1876, moved into the old Pennsylvania Railroad freight depot at Thirteenth and Market. A devout Christian himself, Wanamaker shared Isaac and Justus's adoption of a one-price policy and was quoted as saying, "If everyone was equal before God, then everyone should be equal before price."[9] Wanamaker called his new location the Grand Depot; the store was an impressive structure and had the reputation of being the nation's largest men's and children's clothing store at the time.[10] Wanamaker's, as shoppers referred to it, would prove to be S&C's toughest competitor over the course of the next century. (George Stockton Strawbridge, who became president of S&C in 1955, would frequently command the company's top executives to "get Wanamakers!") The 1870s also saw Lit Brothers set up shop at the northeast corner of Eighth and Market and Snellenberg and Co. at Ninth and Market. Gimbels also made room for itself on the block. As the later part of the nineteenth century ensued, Philadelphia was quickly developing a reputation as one of the birthplaces of modern-day retailing.

What set S&C apart from the competition during its lifetime was its commitment to its founding Quaker principles and its belief in family, both the founding family members and the employees who immediately became part of the family when they were hired.

> *The upper management knew the names of so many employees, from buyers to sales Associates. If I encountered one of them on the elevator or elsewhere, I was greeted by my name. As large as the company was, one nonetheless had this feeling that we were a part of a big family, and this was a nice feeling for myself and many others.*
> —*Barbara McNutt, S&C stationery buyer*[11]

HERBERT TILY

Herbert Tily, one of S&C's most influential employees, represented the very essence of the company's broad definition of "family." He was thirteen when he joined S&C as a messenger boy in 1879 and was paid two dollars a week. Herbert studied accounting in his free time, which eventually landed him a position in the store's accounting department and then the role of chief accountant. By 1905, he was the store's general manager; he became a partner in 1918, vice president and director in 1922 and president in 1927. Herbert's contribution to the store extended far beyond his job titles, though. He had a passion for music and led the store chorus, which started in 1904. He suggested creating a Quarter Century Club to honor employees who had been with the company for twenty-five years or more. He was the visionary behind many of the store's initiatives, including the store's iconic Seal of Confidence, Clover Day, its first branch store and modern employee training programs. Herbert's fervent commitment to

Sketch of Herbert J. Tily from S&C's seventy-five-year commemoration booklet. *Courtesy of the author.*

his S&C family was highlighted at an honorary dinner in 1929 celebrating his fifty years of service to the store. When accepting his recognition, he humbly asked that the entire store be honored and not just him. "Any man to achieve success must have the loyal support of his associates."

Herbert reiterated this sentiment again shortly before his death in 1948, when he confided to Dwight Perkins, his successor as president of the company, "The success of any great business depended more than anything else on the success and happiness of its employees.... The final objective of all business must be to benefit mankind."[12]

On the day of Herbert's funeral in January 1949, all S&C stores closed to honor his life and his sixty-nine years of devoted service.

CHAPTER 2

A GROWING FAMILY, PART I

Becoming a Department Store in a New Age

It is the avowed purpose of good merchants not only to pay people what they are worth, but to assume full responsibility for training them to be worth more.
—*Herbert Tily*

When Strawbridge & Clothier first opened its doors to the public on that summer day in 1868, the store had a staff of thirty. According to Alfred Lief and written accounts by some of the first employees, the staff was primarily composed of Justus and Isaac; buying assistants; salespeople; a bookkeeper; Justus's younger brother, George, as store manager; and cash boys. Since cash registers had not yet been invented—the cash register first appeared in 1883, thanks to the ingenuity of James Ritty, a saloonkeeper in Ohio[13]—cash boys, also called messenger boys, were vital to the sales process. Typically hired at age thirteen or fourteen, these presumably athletic youth ran purchases from the sales counters to the store's two wrapping desks and two cashiers, which were located on the main level and basement level, respectively. The boys would then return the wrapped item along with any change to the customer at the sales desk. Cash boys were also expected to arrive at the store early in the morning to sweep and clean and perform odd jobs. When they were done with their shifts in the evening, they delivered any remaining packages that had not been sent out for home delivery during the day.[14] Most customers took their items with them in those days, but the store did have one horse-drawn carriage that made two delivery trips a day to homes north

Cash girls, 1907. *Courtesy of the Hagley Museum and Library.*

of Market Street and once a day to homes south of Market Street during the fall, winter and spring. During Philadelphia's notoriously humid summers, the store relied on cash boys to carry deliveries during the day, packages strapped to their backs, rather than expose the horses to the sweltering heat. Although this seems harsh by today's standards, it's fair to say that cash boys were not viewed as expendable. Rather, as demonstrated by Herbert Tily's career path, the store's treatment of the boys exemplified its long-running commitment to employee retention and promotion. Benjamin Strawbridge, Justus's older brother, who was superintendent in the 1870s and in charge of most of the hiring, made it a priority to hire boys who "would stay with the house."[15] Similarly to the boys, cash girls, also called messenger girls, were hired to run errands and perform odd jobs, although it is unclear if they delivered packages.

In 1875, the first of several expansions took place, as the store acquired the property at 805 Market Street.[16] In 1878, it acquired buildings at 807 and 809, demolished them along with 805 and erected a new ninety-by-ninety-six-foot building that boasted an elevator shoppers could ride to the second floor, a technological marvel at the time and one of the earliest in the city.

I can remember now seeing the hollows worn in the steps by the shoppers going up and down, a strong evidence of the popularity of the store in those days, when there were no elevators.
—*George W. Stevens, who started as a cash boy at S&C in 1876* [17]

By the 1870s, the store had grown to 278 employees. New departments had been added to keep up with the expanding merchandise. More buyers were employed who were making trips to Europe to purchase "the latest novelties in the most desirable fabrics." [18] Marseilles quilts and handkerchiefs, merino and silk underwear and kid gloves from Grenoble, France, lined the shelves. [19]

Efforts to limit child labor in the United States or end it entirely extend back to the 1830s and were made by various labor associations, unions, child advocates and state legislatures. It wasn't until 1949 that the practice was finally prohibited under an amendment to the Fair Labor Standards Act, signed by President Franklin D. Roosevelt.* S&C ended its use of cash boys and girls in the early 1920s with the permanent installation of cash registers and a pneumatic tube system.†

By the mid-1880s, a mere ten years later, the number of employees had grown to a remarkable two thousand. [20] The mail order department stood at forty employees and distributed a few thousand copies of the *Strawbridge & Clothier Quarterly* a year to homes. There were now forty drivers for the store's horse-drawn wagons to deliver purchases free of charge to Center City homes and to the railroad depots for customers who lived outside of the city. Wagons were painted a dark green with the S&C name displayed in vermilion. The drivers wore custom uniforms and steered dapple-gray horses that were personally chosen by one of Justus's five sons, Frederic Strawbridge, and on which no whips were ever used. [21] "In those days a driver or keeper discovered in any act of cruelty to a horse was instantly dismissed." [22]

S&C's rapid growth reflected a larger national trend among retailers. No longer staffed by a collegial group of employees, many had become multilevel, multidepartment corporations. In fact, it was in the 1890s that such stores began to be commonly referred to as *department stores*, distinguishing them from smaller dry goods and specialty stores. [23] Employees who had started with S&C in its infancy fondly reminisced about the formerly close-knit culture in a special issue

---

* History.com Editors, "Child Labor," History.com, accessed June 10, 2022, https://www.history.com/topics/industrial-revolution/child-labor.
† Lief, *Family Business*, 149–51.

Horse-drawn S&C delivery carriage, 1910/1911. *Courtesy of the Hagley Museum and Library.*

of the monthly employee newsletter, *Store Chat*, that celebrated the store's fiftieth anniversary:

> *We are referred to now as a Store Family. It was then more truly a fact, as each one connected with the house—I think I might say the Firm as well as the employes* [sic]*—was intimately acquainted with each another; their domestic affairs, finances, love affairs, sorrows and all matters pertaining to one's life that would interest his or her immediate family.*
> *—William M. Eisenbrey, employed as an errand boy in 1872*[24]

Charles W. Garman, who began his forty-year career at S&C in 1878 as a monitor for the cash boys, remembered being seriously ill with typhoid, "and for several weeks during the most critical period of my illness, Mr. Strawbridge sent a messenger to my home in Camden each morning and made personal inquiry of my condition. Being but a boy, it was cheering to know that in the midst of great business responsibilities and cares I was so kindly remembered by my employers."[25]

"MRS. CONSUMER"

Retail's historic growth can be largely attributed to remarkable innovation that occurred in the late nineteenth and early twentieth centuries. Incandescent lighting, which Thomas Edison had introduced in 1879, allowed stores to show off their merchandise in a new way, attracting the eyes of more customers. The automobile was replacing horse-drawn carriages. By 1909, S&C had purchased several automobiles for long-distance deliveries to the growing suburbs, while still relying on horse-drawn wagons for Center City deliveries. In all, there were 300 horses, 150 wagons and trucks and 21 automobile delivery trucks.[26]

It was the dawn of a new era in commerce and consumerism with more mass-produced goods, more disposable income and more time to buy, especially for white upper and middle-class women. Department stores turned their attention to this new consumer, who by the 1920s was being referred to as "Mrs. Consumer."[27] Retail historian Vicki Howard says in her book *From Main Street to Mall: The Rise and Fall of the American Department Store* that by the 1890s, department stores became an "Adamless Eden." They evolved into a haven

S&C delivery truck with drivers, 1916. *Courtesy of the Hagley Museum and Library.*

29

for women in the city to shop, rest and socialize. A welcome change, as it wasn't long before that it was considered improper for a woman to venture out into the city unaccompanied by a man.

Department stores also provided a new source of employment for women that was considered socially respectable. For the first several years after S&C opened its doors, most sales staff members were men, as were the buyers. According to George W. Stevens, who started as a cash boy at S&C in 1876, there were only six saleswomen and one woman buyer.[28] Although S&C did not officially track such data at the time, it is safe to assume that in just a few short years, the store, like most U.S. retailers, saw a dramatic increase in the number of women employees. Nationally, "the number of saleswomen jumped from under eight thousand in 1880 to over fifty-eight thousand in 1890."[29] Again, this change favored white women. Few Black women held jobs as sales staff, instead occupying such behind-the-scenes jobs as housekeeping.

The topic of race in department store employment is explored in greater detail in chapter 10, "Responding to Changing Times."

SPECIAL TOUCHES

Perhaps driven by the growing need to cater to "Mrs. Consumer," Strawbridge & Clothier was constantly reassessing the look and feel of its store. It strove to create a more comfortable and welcoming environment that was a far cry from the dimly lit, cramped store of 1868. In 1886, it underwent a renovation after purchasing property at 811–815 Market Street. The local Philadelphia newspapers called the end result a "business palace."[30] The main arcade welcomed an abundance of natural light from the ceiling's skylights and was flanked on either side by grand pillars, incandescent lights and shiny mahogany countertops. There were now seven passenger elevators to help with traffic flow between the first and second floors. The need to have cash boys running about, to the annoyance of customers, was minimized now that the cashiers and package wrappers performed their work in balcony offices, away from the shopping floor: "From their lofty heights the wire baskets which carry the packages are constantly racing to and fro."[31] Always in competition with Wanamaker's and its Grand Depot, S&C declared it was "the Largest Store in the United States devoted exclusively to DRY GOODS."[32] By 1898, the store had succeeded in occupying more than half

Postcard of S&C dress goods aisle at Eighth and Market Street store, 1886. *Courtesy of the Hagley Museum and Library.*

Soda fountain at Eighth and Market Street store, 1905. From the *Glimpses of Strawbridge & Clothier: Great Department Store* booklet, 1905. *Courtesy of the author.*

of the block at Eighth and Market Street with its combined "east, center, and west" stores.[33] More consumer comforts were added, such as women's parlors with attached toilet rooms. Here, shoppers could relax in comfortable chairs, write letters on stationery that was provided and read from a selection of newspapers and magazines. Customers could also enjoy a new candy counter and lunchroom, along with a large soda and ice cream fountain. In fact, milk and cream for the ice cream came from the Moorestown, New Jersey farm of Justus's son Edward Strawbridge.[34]

THE EVOLUTION OF SALESCLERKS: CONDUCT AND TRAINING

When S&C started, men and women worked at the sales counter from eight o'clock in the morning to six o'clock in the evening Monday through Saturday. They were expected to be stationed at their counter when the morning gong sounded.[35] Closing time was known as "cover up," which Justus Strawbridge announced across the store.[36] Later, a closing gong was used. Employees could take forty-five minutes for lunch. William M. Eisenbrey recalled in *Store Chat* that employees were allowed a couple of holidays and vacation time in the early days of the store, "Christmas and Fourth of July being our only full holidays and half a day Thanksgiving. We had two weeks' vacation in the summertime."[37]

Men wore vests, and women wore wrist-length sleeves in black or white with black skirts, even in the warm summer months. Women could also wear black dresses from October to May and light-colored dresses from May through September.

Employee conduct was established in a Book of Rules during the 1880s, which, among other things, instructed that "reading and gossiping during business hours are strictly prohibited."[38] The Book of Rules acted as a self-governing measure by employees. According to William M. Eisenbrey's memory, "Mr. Clothier said that the Firm never made a rule—the employes [*sic*] made the rules."[39]

During the late 1800s and early 1900s, the job of salesclerk was not held in high regard by society. Salesmen and women were often the butt of jokes, referred to as "counter jumpers" and made fun of in newspaper comic strips.[40] Salesclerk was regarded as a low-status job, and the opportunities for growth were not widely recognized. Yet it was undeniable that department stores were

The S&C dress code would, of course, go on to change over the decades, so that by the 1980s and 1990s, the employee handbook advised that women wear dresses, pantsuits and coordinated separates and for hosiery to be worn at all times. For men, it was suits, sports jackets and slacks with shirts and ties. For people working in non-customer-facing positions, a professional appearance was also required, including "jeans that are neat" for people working in stock.

Women couldn't wear slacks. When that rule ended in the early 1970s, many of us never looked back. We're never wearing a dress again.
—Sandra Jackson, copy chief, Advertising Department, 1968–81*

_____

* Sandra Jackson, in discussion with the author, June 2021.

a growing sector feeding the economy. This brought an increasing need for structure, standards and employee training and development, which added to a sense of professionalism. In truth, as retail historian Nancy Koehn points out, the job was never going to get you rich, and the hours were long. But by the mid-1900s, if you worked at one of these stores, "you are well trained. You are well dressed. You have some kind of benefits. You have vacation days. And you can expect that you can work there on a set schedule that you worked out with your manager for many, many years."[41]

By 1910, Herbert Tily, who was now general manager, recognized the changes occurring in the modern business world with its emphasis on standards and efficiency. He observed that "twenty-five years ago in most business institutions a boy was given a position and worked out his own salvation. Today it is different. The institution that does not recognize that its employees must be trained cannot exist."[42]

Training was essential on two fronts: to ensure the store continued to provide its customers with quality trustworthy service and knowledge about its extensive merchandise and to sustain a strong Store Family with high employee retention.

These expectations led to the formation of the Noonday Club for women employees in April 1910. Alfred Lief refers to this as an "elementary" approach to training, since the word "training" wasn't used to describe it. Instead, it was thought of as an educational program driven by the belief that self-improvement led to professional growth and success. It met at twelve thirty for half an hour each day and was developed and managed by women employees. A variety of lessons were offered that coupled business training with more general educational and skill-building opportunities. Some of the initial lessons in that first year were about business arithmetic,

250 Ambitious Girls and Women Wanted at Once

¶ Girls and Women who wish to get on in the world and make a success of their business.

¶ Girls and Women eager to learn—to further their education along one line or many.

¶ Girls and Women with talents to develop and turn to account.

¶ Girls and Women who aspire to gentle arts and the qualities of culture.

¶ Girls and Women who long for social life or the good hand of fellowship.

¶ Girls and Women who are naturally "good fellows" or want to be; who are willing to help or be helped.

Apply to the Noon Day Club
The Latch String is Always Out

NOTE:—We need two hundred and fifty to double our membership before that next Big Event. Now, aren't you curious? Fifty cents will put you right with the rest of us, and not even a Clover Day Bargain would bring you so much for your money. Ask Miss Lynch, Notion Department, for particulars.

Left: Noonday Club advertisement in a 1913 issue of *Store Chat*. *Courtesy of the author.*

Below: S&C junior students and two of their teachers, 1912. *Courtesy of the author.*

salesmanship, grammar, history and interpretation of literature. Embroidery and crocheting—referred to as "the gentle arts" in a 1913 issue of *Store Chat*—were also taught. A schoolroom was set up on the fourth floor to host lessons that were taught by fellow employees who volunteered to share their expertise. As reported in the December 1910 issue of *Store Chat*, "Eighty-two young women have given at least one-half hour of their noon rest periods to some form of study.…The club is entirely controlled by its members and classes arranged largely by request."

For young men, including cash boys, a Department of Instruction was created that offered classes twice a week for two hours on penmanship, spelling, store deportment and gymnastics.[43] Employee physical fitness was of great importance to the company, which believed that a sharp mind and a strong body contributed to productivity.

Continuing education was important even for those who opted out of school. By 1912, there were 275 boys and girls younger than sixteen who had left school to earn a wage at S&C.[44] The store required them to attend a junior school six mornings a week in addition to their regular work. Most of the youth had left school between the third grade and first year of high school. They were placed in classes that were their grade-level equivalent, picking up where they left off.

That same year saw the introduction of S&C's Commercial Efficiency course, later recognized as the first employee training program in the country.[45] The program was open to both men and women who wished to pursue executive-level positions; S&C was the only department store in the city to offer this training to women.[46] Graduates of the course proudly received a diploma. For employees who were not on the executive-level career path, an intermediate school was created. This provided training for positions as bill checkers and for work involving ledgers and selling.[47] Regardless of an employee's career path, there was no advancement without completing the training and passing a test.

A revised Book of Rules was also issued in 1912. Compiled by management, it included sixty rules that covered personal conduct, discipline, store systems and established expectations for employee-customer relations. It's clear that management felt it was still important that the rules not be rigid "top down" declarations. An article from *Store Chat* declared that the new Book of Rules "stands in a class alone as compared with similar Books issued by other stores, in that [it] is more liberal in its rules, and does not so minutely regulate the conduct of employes [*sic*]." In fact, management welcomed employees to challenge any rule they found

Top: A buyer holds a merchandise meeting with salespeople in the China and Glassware Department, 1931. *Courtesy of the Hagley Museum and Library.*

Bottom: Sponsors working with new salespeople, 1962. *Courtesy of the Hagley Museum and Library.*

"unnecessary, unwise or unjust," in which case, the rule would be reviewed and changed if proven to be any one of these.[48]

In 1919, what had been called the Employment Bureau was changed to the Personnel Department and began operating as part of the Operations Department. Alfred Lief notes that the store officially began referring to its educational work as "training" at this time. S&C had adopted the belief that the Store "was a great school in which the department heads, as faculty, had responsibility for bringing out the abilities of their people."[49] By the early 1930s, the Training Department had the slogan "Every employee a student" and encouraged members of the Store Family to build toward new opportunities within the company.

Buyers were instrumental to trainings. Tily strongly emphasized that they were responsible for the records of their salespeople.[50] In the mornings before the store opened, routine meetings were held around the sales counter for buyers to teach their salespeople about the merchandise. Visits to suppliers' factories were also arranged for salespeople.

The Sponsor Association, which formed in 1920, provided training and guidance from older employees (sponsors) to new hires. Sponsors reviewed roles and responsibilities with new hires, introduced them to their colleagues and welcomed them to the Store Family. The Sponsor Association existed for the duration of the company.

Seal of Confidence

In the early days of S&C, Justus and Isaac and the original salespeople knew many of their customers and often extended a handshake at the end of a sale, both as a form of congeniality and an affirmation

The original Seal of Confidence, 1911.

The 1968 Centennial medallion.

Modification adopted in 1944.

Changes to the Seal of Confidence over the years. *Courtesy of the author.*

of a trustworthy transaction. This practice became impractical as the store grew. Perhaps in honor of Justus Strawbridge, who had died in March 1911, Herbert Tily, then the store's general manager, proposed a trademark that would more effectively capture the mutual regard between customer and salesperson. Tily conceived of what would become S&C's iconic Seal of Confidence. The design was inspired by the legendary handshake between Pennsylvania's Quaker founder, William Penn, and Chief Tamanend of the Lenni-Lenape tribe, the original inhabitants of the land.

The seal was registered on November 21, 1911, and would be imprinted on all S&C storefronts, marketing and promotional materials, letterheads, gift boxes and more. New salespeople were taught that they were integral to the store and were instructed by Tily "to be absolutely true and just in all your dealings with the public."[51] Isaac Clothier Jr. instructed buyers and executives at a dinner meeting that "it is incumbent upon you to see that every article brought into the store is worthy of this Seal."[52]

History has shown how quickly treaties between colonial governments and tribal governments became broken promises as the colonialist population grew along with its desire for land and resources. Although William Penn and Chief Tamanend's treaty resulted in what is called the "Great Treaty"*—nearly fifty years of good relations—it, too, eventually succumbed to the greed of Penn's descendants. To this day, Pennsylvania does not recognize its Indigenous tribes.

---

* Andrew Newman, "Treaty of Shackamaxon," The Encyclopedia of Greater Philadelphia, accessed January 31, 2023. https://philadelphiaencyclopedia.org/essays/treaty-of-shackamaxon-2/.

The ethos embodied by the seal remained important to all employees throughout the life of the company. An employee handbook from 1987 emphasizes, "Our Store symbol, the Seal of Confidence is a pledge of fair dealing to all our customers, our suppliers, and to you, our Associates." This commitment to customer service contributed to national accolades. In 1993, the company was ranked the number one leader in customer satisfaction by the Retail Satisfaction Index.[53]

Time and again, this commitment was put into practice, as highlighted by these comical and touching S&C employee-customer experiences:

Ray Pascali
Sales Associate, 1979–84

Although I primarily worked in the men's department, it was not uncommon for me to relieve co-workers from other departments. It was in the men's sleep ware department where I had a very bizarre encounter. An elderly lady had approached me with a pair of pajamas that she wished to return. Normally this would be no big deal if the nightwear was the wrong size, or an undesirable color, but I was appalled when I heard the elderly lady's reason for the return—she no longer needed the pajamas because her husband had died in them! I stood shocked at the register when the service manager instructed me to accept the return. This transaction gave liberal return policy a whole new meaning.

I realized later the trust that they gained in customers benefitted the store in the long run. It was passed down generation to generation. It's what made the store so successful. The Seal of Confidence.[54]

Another guy would come in from the Tioga neighborhood. He came in with his sister. I think he was lonely. He would come by my counter and ask to see different wallets. He never bought anything. I would spend time with him. He was courteous.[55]

Clem Pascarella
Stock Office, 1977–89

Strawbridge's took anything back. A customer came in with a package of men's T-shirts that were clearly marked on the package: "Sears." I was told we take everything back. They took the receipt from the customer and reimbursed her. Who knows where the T-shirts went at that point.[56]

Reverend Joseph W. Bongard
Service Manager, 1977–85

Father Bongard remembers being allowed to give a woman car fare to get home when she came in very upset because she had lost her wallet. "That's what the store would do, that extra mile. I think that's why people liked shopping there. They were really being served."[57]

CHAPTER 3

A GROWING FAMILY, PART II

A New Structure and a New Generation

THE EMERGING SCIENCE OF RETAIL

By the 1920s, department stores were the epicenter of affordable mass-produced goods for middle-class families across the country. As retail historian Vicki Howard describes, "they had come to stand for the might of American capitalism and the democracy of goods."[58] Most major cities and even smaller towns could boast their own department store, often a grand building, centrally located, that stood as a source of regional pride. While riding this wave of capitalist growth, many department stores felt it was in their interest to transition from privately owned companies to publicly traded ones. Macy's and Gimbels became incorporated in 1922. When S&C's annual sales for that year exceeded $26 million, giving it the status of a large enterprise, it filed for incorporation, as well.[59]

A large enterprise needed greater standardization and stability. Toward the end of the nineteenth century, retailers started to track market statistics and share practices through the formation of local trade organizations. By 1911, the National Retail Dry Goods Association (NRDGA) had been created to further standardize data.[60] World War I brought higher taxes, which prompted stores to improve their expense accounting. Many started working with outside business experts. Harvard's Bureau of Business Research became very involved in the industry. The NRDGA funded some

Staff Council, 1928. *Courtesy of the Hagley Museum and Library.*

of their research. Stores adopted new scientific management techniques to eliminate wasteful practices and plan store expansions.[61]

The Retail Research Association had also formed in 1916 as a cooperative of small retailers to share figures on operating expenses and profits. It was renamed the Associated Merchandise Corporation (AMC) in 1918 with the new purpose of pooling buying power to help smaller retailers compete against big chains like Sears.[62] In 1923, S&C became a member and soon adopted the AMC's new scientific research when it decided to organize all selling departments under eight divisional merchandise managers. Previously, Isaac Clothier Jr. had been general merchandise manager overseeing all departments, but the job was becoming too complex as more and more departments were created. The result of the reorganization was positive. Greater control and planning around merchandise buying led to increased profits in 1925.

S&C also recognized the need to maintain personal contact and communication between the growing number of employees (which were several thousand now) and management. In 1928, the Staff Council was created. An article in the June 1928 *Store Chat* issue touted that "neither Employe nor Management can attain a full measure of success without the

After the deaths of Justus in 1911 and Isaac in 1921, Morris Clothier and Isaac H. Clothier Jr. ran the company. Justus's sons Francis, Frederic and Robert served as partners in the firm. The partners transitioned to board directors when S&C became a publicly traded company. Morris was elected president, Isaac was VP and treasurer, Francis Strawbridge was VP and secretary and Herbert Tily was VP.[*]

_____

* Lief, *Family Business*, 156.

happy co-operation of the other." Meeting monthly, the council was composed of thirty representatives who were elected by employees and two who were appointed by management. At the council's first meeting, the representatives voted to increase the employee discount from 10 to 20 percent for most retail items; it remained at 20 percent until 1996. All S&C and, later, Clover employees, no matter their position in the company, benefitted from an employee discount. The council lasted just over two decades, addressing employee and managerial relations. When the Personnel Department established itself as an independent department in the 1950s, there was no longer a need for the council, which subsequently dissolved.

A NEW GENERATION AND THE RISE OF THE EXECUTIVE DEVELOPMENT PROGRAM

After surviving the economic toll of the Great Depression and the uncertainty and human toll of two world wars, S&C entered a new stage of growth and evolution in the 1950s that continued into the 1980s.

Piloting this ascent in 1955 was George Stockton Strawbridge, the first member of the Strawbridge family to be elected president of the company. Previously, the company had been co-led by its founders, followed by Isaac's son, Morris Clothier, then the multitalented Herbert Tily and, later, Dwight Perkins.

Stockton reluctantly entered the family business in 1934. His passion was in aviation, not retail. He wanted to become a commercial pilot, but after he obtained his transport pilot's license, he found there were few jobs to be had. As a young man, he worked his way through multiple layers of the company, including stock boy, salesman and clerk, before finally becoming a buyer of junior dresses. When World War II broke out, he left retail to put his love of flying to use as a naval aviator, serving as a plane commander in the Naval Air Transport Service. After four years of service, he accepted an offer to return to S&C in 1946 to become the divisional merchandise manager

G. Stockton Strawbridge with his son Peter during World War II. *Courtesy of the author.*

for the new ready-to-wear division. Stockton was eager to spice things up with the store's fashion merchandise, which he viewed as dull. "Our ready-to-wear floor could be characterized as appealing to middle-aged Quaker ladies buying with confidence what we had to sell, and not to the attractive young woman."[63] From ready-to-wear, he was off and running. A visionary, Stockton wasn't afraid of taking risks in pursuit of progress and innovation, yet he was also mindful of when to move cautiously. His love for the family business was unquestionable, as was his love for its employees. He shared Herbert Tily's belief that a business's success depends on the success of its people. Like his grandfather Justus, he valued trust and honesty.

With the historic rise of the middle class after World War II, more Americans had more spending money. Between 1940 and 1965, the average family income in the United States nearly tripled. Between 1950 and 1970, poverty declined by more than 60 percent.[64] Retailers responded to this tremendous demographic change by becoming more homogenous. Whatever had distinguished them from each other before was now blurred. Stores carried similar merchandise and offered similar services and operating hours. For S&C to stand out in this new climate, the company turned to its employees. It invested more in recruiting qualified personnel. As Alfred Lief notes, "Strawbridge & Clothier believed it spent more money selecting, training, and guiding people than any other department store in town, and its turnover rate was comparatively low."[65]

Stockton was keenly wise to the way in which training would help the store meet the competition of a growing postwar retail industry. Early on in his presidency, the Personnel Department separated from Operations and became its own independent department to handle all personnel training.[66] Stockton also revived the Executive Development Program, which had started in 1930 but fizzled during World War II. The program was an updated version of the earlier Commercial Efficiency course. It was open to any current S&C employee who had a college degree and wished to become a buyer, an executive-level position. To apply, they would have to undergo an interview and receive approval. It was important that employees understood the commitment they were making and possessed the traits that would push them to success—or, as Stockton put it, anyone who had a "zest for conflict," which he defined as a "highly competitive drive to accomplish."[67] The program was nine months long, with a starting position of assistant buyer. Participants benefitted from on-the-job training with nearly one hundred hours of classroom time and seminars taught by the company's top management and VPs. Walt Cleaver, who worked for

Executive Development Program graduates, 1958. *Courtesy of the author.*

Executive Development Program graduates, 1987. *Courtesy of the author.*

S&C from 1971 to 1996 and became the director of employee relations and organization development, felt that it was this buy-in by top management that made the program successful. Seminars covered all aspects of the business, including merchandising, operations, advertising and personnel. After completing the program, participants were on the path to becoming buyers, a position they typically achieved within a four- to five-year period. Thirty to forty participants graduated each year. A special luncheon was held in the Corinthian Room with guest speakers that included reputable business leaders such as John Haas, chairman of Rohm & Haas; Ralph Roberts, founder and CEO of Comcast; and elected officials. By the 1970s, the program had expanded to Clover division employees, and by 1985, the company proudly reported that 95 percent of its buyers were promoted from within.[68]

While Sales Associates and other S&C employees were encouraged to enroll in the program, the company also devoted much time and resources to annual college recruitment efforts. S&C representatives visited campuses throughout the Delaware Valley and up and down the Eastern Seaboard in search of graduates eager to begin a career in retail. "The program was considered to be the best in the retail business," said Walt Cleaver.

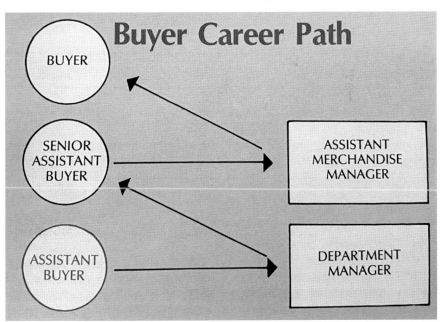

Diagram of a buyer's career path at S&C, 1970s. *Courtesy of the Hagley Museum and Library.*

For employees who were not interested in the merchandise side of the company but wished to pursue opportunities in the store's operations, a Basic Retail Program was developed in the early 1960s.[69] Participants came recommended by their supervisors and enrolled in a nine-month-long program from September to May. Classes were held each Friday and focused on supervisory skills, basic retail math like markups and markdowns, how to pay vendors and personal development. On completion of the course, an employee was eligible to become a branch store manager or a divisional manager, which, like a buyer, was considered an executive-level position.

Sales Associates also had ongoing training once a season to learn about new merchandise and meet with vendors. To help improve customer service, the Secret Shopper Program was developed in the early 1980s. Undercover shoppers would go to different branch stores and test the customer service of the Sales Associates in the field, praising those who did well and working with those who needed extra help.

The 1960s brought a fourth generation of Strawbridges who wanted to pursue careers in the family business. (Isaac Clothier IV, who represented the fourth generation of the Clothiers, never worked at the store but was elected board member in 1975.) Stockton made sure that Justus and Isaac's progeny did not escape the store's high standards for employment. A special training program was established for the new generation, which

Basic Retail Program graduates, 1994. *Courtesy of the author.*

Stockton and the fourth generation. *From left*: Francis, Peter, Stockton, Steven, David. 1968. *Courtesy of the author.*

included Francis, Peter, David and Steven Strawbridge. Requirements were a college degree, spending one year at a fellow AMC store and participating in that store's executive development course. If the trainees completed the course and performed well, they could then participate in S&C's Executive Development Program. All four Strawbridge family members completed the program and became buyers. They remained with the company for over twenty-five years, eventually filling its highest executive ranks and guiding it through its final decades.

David Strawbridge, vice president of personnel, recalls that his uncle "Stock" started the program to avoid hiring a family member who might not perform well or decide that retail wasn't for them and quit. Stock felt it was important to have at least one year of retail experience before joining S&C, explained David, adding, "I think we all benefitted from it. It was kind of fun."

BUYERS

Although every position with the store was critical to its success, the role of buyer was particularly unique. It was a position that required deep knowledge of specific merchandise as well as expertise in how merchandise was manufactured and the trends driving its popularity.

S&C's Paris office, 1910. *Courtesy of the Hagley Museum and Library.*

From 1868 until 1923, S&C organized its own buying trips, sending buyers to meet with manufacturers in New York and Boston, as well as major European fashion and textile centers. They even traveled to cities in Asia. In the age before commercial air travel, trips were made by boat and train and would last months. One buyer, a Mr. Walsh, left on Washington's birthday and returned by Easter.[70]

In 1904, the store opened an office in Paris, which provided lodging for S&C buyers and a permanent staff to arrange meetings with manufacturers. Eventually, the company would have offices in London, Vienna, Berlin and New York.[71] Announcements about buying trips were shared in *Store Chat*. In the June 1906 issue, employees read about the excursions of four S&C buyers who left by boat to Europe for "jewelry, watches, silver and objets d'art." They traveled to France, Germany, Holland, Austria, Switzerland and Italy. One whimsical account read, "Here's something odd: This is Mr. Beck's thirteenth trip abroad. His first trip he made on August 13, 1894 (last year he went twice). Aisle 13 is in his department. The house from which he recently moved was numbered 1713; the house into which he has moved is 113. Mr. Beck says 13 is his lucky number."[72]

By 1923, it was clear that running international offices came at a greater expense than shareholders might like. The newly incorporated store decided to close its European offices and instead invest in what would become a long-lasting and highly beneficial membership to the AMC. In addition to providing well-researched data and analysis on operational standards, AMC staff planned the itineraries for S&C buyers and arranged tours with small and large manufacturers throughout Europe and Asia.

Betsy Horen
S&C Handbag Buyer

Betsy Horen was the S&C buyer for handbags and small leather goods from the 1970s until the company closed. She is fondly remembered by many S&C employees and customers for lovingly but firmly explaining that "you read a book, you purse your lips, you carry a *handbag*."

Betsy recalls the numerous questions and countless variables she would have to consider when completing her six-month plans for her supervisor. "What sold well; what didn't? What do you need to order more of; what do you need to get rid of? What met your expectations; what didn't? What needed to be marked down? What happens if what you mark down does really badly and it uses more of your markdown money than you want?"

She also recalls how critical it was for a buyer to possess a keen understanding of the store's customer base and customers' regional and economic differences. As S&C developed branch locations, the tastes and needs of its customers varied from branch to branch. "Cherry Hill had a very wealthy customer. King of Prussia had a wealthy customer. Willow Grove, too. Jenkintown was a Maine Line customer who could have had money but wouldn't buy higher-priced items. You knew who your customer was. You didn't need to know what the fashion was or understand it; you just had to have it in your department."

Betsy Horen. *Courtesy of Betsy Horen.*

Perhaps the more glamorous part of Betsy's job was the travel. She frequently traveled to Europe to pick out merchandise. Starting in London, she would buy LOL bags: "little old lady bags, the kind Queen Elizabeth has." After London, she went to Paris. "The prices would go up there, but it was more fashionable." From Paris, she flew to Germany for small leather goods that were beautifully made. Then she went to Florence, Italy, where she spent an entire week. The AMC would schedule daytime visits to manufacturers. In the evenings, she would go out to dinner with her AMC representatives and with buyers from other stores. The opportunities to get to know AMC staff on a more personal level, as well as the manufacturers and buyers from other stores, were what she treasured most about her trips. "It was wonderful. You really met Italians, and the manufacturers. They became your best friends. My relationships over there haven't ended."

A people person by nature, Betsy treasured the social aspect of being a buyer, interacting not just with her manufacturers and AMC reps but also with her team of Sales Associates, her divisional merchandise manager and, of course, the customers. She felt at home with the company that she says gave her so much. To this day, she tears up when talking about it. She remains close with her S&C family and close to Eighth and Market. Occasionally, she encounters people who light up when they learn that she once worked for Strawbridge & Clothier. The memories come pouring out, and she welcomes them.[73]

Barbara McNutt
S&C Stationery Buyer

Barbara entered the Executive Development Program at S&C in 1972, fresh out of college. She almost didn't last her first year. Working under Gertrude Sickler, the buyer for the Gift Department, proved trying. Although Gertrude had a reputation for excellent taste in merchandise, she also had a reputation for being very volatile and temperamental. "One minute she would be screaming at you on the selling floor in front of customers, and the next minute she would compliment your blouse," said Barbara. Fortunately, Barbara quickly moved on to other departments and in 1978 became the buyer for Stationery. "Those were my most memorable and happy experiences." She has especially fond memories of working with John Kreemer, her divisional merchandise manager. He was an older man with a long S&C career. Barbara remembers him as very kind, helpful and full of good advice. He liked to say during their annual reviews that he gave her "guidance and direction."

Barbara enjoyed buying trips abroad and said that all the buyers and upper management were treated to the nicest accommodations. She remembers one trip she took to Germany with Kreemer in 1979. They had a day off from their AMC meetings and decided to see Neuschwanstein Castle. It was February and snowing. "It was so beautiful, like something out of a movie," she said. After touring the castle, they went into the small town and enjoyed some apple strudel and hot cocoa. During their conversation, Kreemer prophesied what was to come. "I want you to enjoy everything that you're doing," he said. "I don't think any of this will exist in ten years."[74] Sadly, his forewarning turned out to be true. When Barbara left the Stationery Department in 1983, the woman who replaced her did not get to travel nearly as much. Tastes had started to change, and interest in certain merchandise was waning. The price of goods had also escalated, making it no longer cost-effective for buyers to travel to certain countries.

Barbara McNutt. *Courtesy of Barbara McNutt.*

Paul Greenholt
Assistant Merchandise Manager

Paul Greenholt. *Courtesy of Paul Greenholt.*

Paul Greenholt didn't even have his driver's license when he started working at S&C's Wilmington, Delaware branch store in 1980. At just sixteen, he was below the company's age requirement of eighteen. However, due to his "trifecta" of connections (his girlfriend's neighbor was the personnel manager for the store, his neighbor was the service manager and his mother was a Sales Associate), he was able to squeak by and secured a part-time job on the selling floor. He enjoyed it so much that he continued to work part time throughout college. Once he graduated, he entered the Executive Development Program. On successfully completing the program, he was invited to a tea and breakfast in the executive offices on the tenth floor of the Eighth and Market Store. He was a nervous twenty-three-year-old with a brand-new briefcase, suit and tie, dressed to impress Stockton Strawbridge—yet all he could think of was, "I have to balance a cup of tea and a Danish without getting it all over me!"

Paul devoted the next eleven years of his early career to the company. During that time, he worked in five different S&C branch stores, including Eighth and Market. He worked his way up to assistant merchandise manager at the Christiana branch store. He was just shy of becoming a buyer before deciding to take a job with QVC in 1992. Along the way, he was nominated several times for the company's Star Associate award, which recognized Associates for their outstanding performance.

"I really enjoyed growing up with the company," said Paul. Not only did he finally get his driver's license during his time at S&C, but he also met his wife (a fellow S&C employee), bought a house and became an expecting father. In fact, he still has some of the furniture he bought with his employee discount.

One of the most important lessons Paul learned from his training was to not forget where you came from. When talking about the many different positions Associates worked on their way to becoming buyers, Paul emphasized, "It's so important to understand what each position does and how they are interrelated and keep the store running."

That and "the customer is always right." This was reinforced by his supervisor, Al Garton, store manager for the Christiana branch store, who told him, "Do what's right. There's nothing you would decide to do to help a customer that I wouldn't agree with." Paul took both lessons with him to QVC and into his next career as a local area real estate professional.[75]

Debbie Herron Jeffreys
Merchandise Information Trainer

Debbie Herron Jeffreys.
Courtesy of Debbie Herron Jeffreys.

When Debbie Herron Jeffreys applied to the Executive Development Program in 1983, she was declined. Feeling brave, she uncharacteristically walked into the Personnel Department at Eighth and Market and told the woman there that S&C had made a mistake and the company should hire her. Soon after, she received a call informing her that she had been accepted. Debbie's bravery took hold again when later, as a department manager for women's shoes, she voiced her concerns to her buyers that some of the Sales Associates were not relating well to customers. She was directed to Walt Cleaver in Personnel, who told her, "You're in the wrong place. We could use someone who really works with people." Always focused on maintaining a reputation for outstanding customer service, the company, at that time, was set on becoming the best in the industry. Debbie could help them get there. From then on, she was the merchandise information trainer and spent the next two years writing customer service training manuals, conducting workshops with Sales Associates, working on the Secret Shopper Program and teaching a "Fiber and Fabrics" class for the Executive Development Program. "I loved everything about my job! I loved that every day was different," she said. Although she had to leave

S&C in 1987 when her husband took a job out of state, she undoubtedly made an impact on both the company culture and its commitment to customer service.[76]

CHAPTER 4

A GROWING FAMILY, PART III

Eighth and Market and Beyond

As a young boy, I was told, anecdotally, that in the late 1940s following World War II and before the advent of branch stores, more business was done daily on the corners of Eighth and Market Streets among Gimbels, Lit Brothers and Strawbridge & Clothier than on any other corner in the United States.
—*Francis R. Strawbridge III, chairman of the board*[77]

By the late 1920s, Market Street was still the dominant retail center for Philadelphia shoppers. S&C, Lit Brothers, Wanamaker's, Snellenburg's, Gimbels and Frank and Seder together made up one-quarter of the city's retail business.[78] S&C's building, at that time, occupied 297 feet on Market Street and extended 306 feet back to Filbert Street. The building was divided into four sections connected by wide doorways and ranged from four to six stories high—impressive but no longer considered modern. Recognizing the value of the building's location and feeling confident of its staying power, S&C officers decided it was time to invest in a monumental reconstruction of the Eighth and Market property. At a board meeting in 1927, chairman Morris Clothier announced plans to rebuild the store. Construction started in 1929 and officially ended in 1932. The result was an impressive thirteen-story building with a penthouse two stories higher that housed the machinery to control the passenger elevators.[79] Made of granite, Indiana limestone and concrete, it was the first department store in the world to be constructed with setbacks (a steplike recession in the wall of a building). It was twice as large as its predecessor, boasting twenty-

The new store at Eighth and Market Street, 1932. *Courtesy of the Hagley Museum and Library.*

seven acres of floor space, which amounted to an increase of 60 percent in selling space. Amazingly, no additional land was acquired for the building.

Shoppers and employees admired and appreciated the modern touches. The new building was the first store in the city to have air conditioning, although it was limited to the basement and first floor. There were twenty passenger elevators that opened to a spacious central lobby on each floor and seven additional elevators in the west section of the building.[80] The building was the first in the city and third in the country to use the Charge-a-Plate, an early form of the credit card that was developed in 1928 and used by large-scale merchants until the 1950s.[81] There were more than three thousand electric lights to attractively showcase merchandise. Public telephone booths were located on all floors.[82] Of particular appeal to employees were the terraces on the eleventh floor, which they took full advantage of during breaks.

> *Last summer…*[the terraces] *were life savers, for one could always find a cool spot….It has to be a pretty stormy day not to find members of the Store Family walking or resting on this aerial rendezvous.*
> —*January 1932 issue of* Store Chat

Despite all the impressive features of the new store (which came at a price tag of nearly $10 million[83]) and a fervent commitment to their Market Street location, president Tily and chairman Clothier saw the writing on the wall. With an increase in automobile ownership, Center City traffic and parking were becoming a bigger headache for retailers. Additionally, suburban expansion increased demand for retailers outside of the city. Tily admitted that "modern conditions of living demand modern methods of merchandising." Branch stores seemed to be the answer.

Although other department stores around the country had established branch locations within their urban boundaries, only a few had branched out into the suburbs: Filene's in Boston, Marshall Fields in Chicago and Bullocks in Los Angeles. In Philadelphia, none of S&C's competitors had expanded into the suburbs.

S&C did not officially cease use of Charge-a Plate cards until February 2, 1968. On that day, thousands of customers were issued new wallet-sized blue plastic S&C charge cards.*

In 1930, two years before completing the remodel of Eighth and Market, S&C welcomed shoppers to its new Ardmore location. As with many of S&C's future branch stores, Ardmore was not just an extension of the flagship store; it was part of the local community. The suburban town sat approximately nine miles west from Center City and rested in the heart of the Main Line, home to some of Philadelphia's prominent old-money families. S&C employee Elfried German, who was tasked with preparing the Ardmore store for its opening, recalled the store's early clientele in a 1980 interview for the *Philadelphia Bulletin*. "They

* *Store Chat* 59, no. 1 (January–February 1968): 4.

wore only riding clothes....If they didn't come on horseback, they arrived in limousines with chauffeurs."[84] Horses were left on the front lawn under the care of the store's doorman. Many customers enjoyed gathering on the porch of the store's mezzanine floor where garden furniture was displayed, giving the store its nickname, "the Ardmore club." S&C opened its second branch location about ten miles north of the city in Jenkintown in 1931.

The simultaneous attempt to modernize the Center City store and keep up with suburban growth, all while a historic depression gripped the nation, took a toll. Profits at Eighth and Market decreased by 8 percent for fiscal year 1931–32 due to the need to lower prices.[85] Although profits from branch stores contributed to overall profits, they were not enough to offset the financial hardships of the Depression. S&C was not alone. Risk-taking ceased among local retailers, making Ardmore and Jenkintown the only branch stores for any department store in the Delaware Valley for twenty years.[86]

This changed in the post–World War II years, when department stores seized on the opportunity to profit from the "pent-up

Market Street continued to be the city's main shopping district well into the 1960s. Betsy Horen recalls that, as a teenager in the early 1960s, she and her friends would begin their shopping at Lit Brothers, move on to S&C, cross the street to Gimbels, walk up Market Street to Blauner's, and then continue on to Snellenburg's, followed by Wanamaker's. From there, they would go to Chestnut Street and test perfume at the cosmetic counter at Dewees' on Thirteenth and Chestnut—then it was on to the Blum store, and finally, they'd end at Bonwit Teller on Chestnut and Seventeenth and admire the hatboxes with purple flowers on them.

demand" that followed decades of economic and political uncertainty. Expansion and modernization were critical. "Those that did not 'chain-up' or expand into the suburbs were seen as 'at risk of becoming an anachronism' due to the rise of discounters, suburban shopping centers and the changing needs and desires of consumers."[87] Between 1950 and 1955, the suburban population grew seven times as fast as the population in city centers.[88] Much of this was tied to cars, sales of which quadrupled across the country between 1946 and 1955.[89]

For many retailers in the postwar era, the future was in branch stores and suburban shopping centers. It didn't make financial sense to update downtown buildings. S&C, motivated by a strong sense of loyalty to its flagship location, followed its own path and did both. In 1946, it updated

S&C Ardmore branch store, 1930. *Courtesy of the Hagley Museum and Library.*

the layout of its fashion floor at Eighth and Market, under the direction of Stockton. Just a few years later, in 1952, the company opened its third branch store in Wilmington, Delaware. S&C would go on to open ten more branch stores spanning southeastern Pennsylvania, New Jersey and northern Delaware by 1996.

The value of branch stores became abundantly clear in 1954 when end-of-year reports showed that, combined, the Ardmore, Jenkintown and Wilmington stores brought in 29 percent of total sales volume. This made up for declining Center City sales. The future of S&C as a multistore operation was summed up by Stockton's 1957 statement to the board, "It has been well said that when a business stops growing it starts dying."[90]

Perhaps the most anticipated branch store opening was in October 1961, when S&C became the anchor store for the new Cherry Hill Shopping Center, the first and largest completely covered and climate-controlled shopping center east of the Mississippi.[91] Nearly three thousand people showed up for the opening.[92] S&C associate Barbara Padgett told the *Philadelphia Inquirer* in 1996 that she remembered opening day: "It was unbelievable. It was wall-

S&C Cherry Hill branch store, 1961. *Courtesy of the Hagley Museum and Library.*

Introducing Our Elevator Department

Don't you like their military bearing "at attention"—and their smiles? We're introducing the department by name, although unfortunately a few were off-duty that day: Helen Behm, Agnes Bryan, Jean Cannon, Louise Clifford, Elizabeth Dolphin, Jane Dowdy, Kathleen Duffy, Isabel Gallagher, Rachel Giordano, Jean Goraj, Stella Goraj, Shirley Jaggard, Jacquelyn Johnston, Beatrice Jones, Frances Keepers, Anna Knupp, Theresa Lovencheck, Kathryn Lehmkuhl, Naomi Long, Margaret McCullion, Anna McGrath, Alyce Madden, Claire Murry, Nellie Murray, Bernice Nelson, Anna O'Connor, Angeline Palma, Sara Perell, Dorothy Phelan, Helen Pieta, Linda Pisani, Adelaide Randall, Catherine Roche, Florence Schlacter, Josephine Schlacter, Carl Smith, Florence Toner, Catherine Toole, Florence Trew, Margaret Wagner.

S&C elevator girls at Eighth and Market store, 1949. *Hagley Museum and Library.*

to-wall people. We stood at the main doors, and when they opened, we had to run back."[93] Cherry Hill would go on to become S&C's most profitable branch store.

Still, the company remained committed to its beloved flagship location. While other department stores like Snellenburg's and Blauner's closed their Center City stores, S&C continued to invest in further modernizing and upgrading the building. Air conditioning was expanded to other floors, and more modern lighting was installed. To meet the ever-increasing demand for parking, S&C partnered with its neighbor Lit Brothers and built the largest parking garage in the city in 1964 (holding nearly one thousand cars on five levels).[94] By the late 1960s, escalators had been revamped and expanded all the way up to the ninth floor. Around the same time, the head-turning elevator girls were replaced by automated elevators.

MEMORIES OF AN ELEVATOR OPERATOR

Nancy Hemsing. *Courtesy of Nancy Hemsing.*

Alfred Lief writes that all the women hired as elevator operators in the 1930s to operate the twenty passenger cars at the new Eighth and Market store were blonde and attractive. It was rumored that they were measured against an outline drawn on a personnel office wall when applying.[95]

Perhaps this practice ended by the 1960s, or perhaps it never took place. Whatever the truth, Nancy Hemsing has no memory of being subjected to such sexist scrutiny when she was hired as an elevator operator in the summer of 1962. Seeking summer work while attending Moore College of Art and Design, she landed the job thanks in part to a good family friend, Henry Hemsing, S&C's general superintendent. (Henry would later become Nancy's father-in-law.)

Training for the job consisted of learning how to manually operate the cars, which involved raising and lowering the large lever to pull open and close the doors and selecting the desired floors for customers on a clocklike dial. Just as important was Nancy's knowledge of the store itself: where all the different departments and the bathrooms were located and the names of all the officers. She had to pass a test where she was shown photographs of each officer and had to identify them by name and title. She was also instructed to politely engage with customers but not be intrusive.

Nancy's uniform was a form-fitting lavender tea-length skirt, a matching jacket with half sleeves and a white blouse. She recalled that the shoes were like old lady shoes. "They were supposed to be very comfortable." Fortunately, Nancy remembers that most people were always very nice—even when she unknowingly bumped against a lever that caused the elevator to stop midway between the basement and first floor with a car full of passengers. They were rescued by an elevator mechanic, who quietly let her know the error she had made without informing the passengers, much to Nancy's relief. "I was very embarrassed," she said. Despite the mishap and her short time at S&C, it was a fun summer job, and she enjoyed being at Eighth and Market. "I loved that place," she said.[96]

No matter how much money was invested into Eighth and Market, it was clear that the company's survival lay in its regional growth. To adapt to this reality, the company made personnel adjustments. The assistant branch manager position was created to share responsibilities with the manager. The assistant would focus on operations while the manager focused on merchandise.

As the chain of command grew, branch managers gained more responsibility and independence. In addition to having a deep knowledge about the branch's merchandise and stock levels and the energy to respond immediately to multiple demands, managers had to possess initiative and be motivated to try new things. They also had to know and understand their clientele. In Cherry Hill and Springfield, for example, a Woman's Advisory Board formed. Composed of "prominent" women from the community (aka Mrs. Consumers), the committee's purpose was "to advise store management with suggestions and constructive criticism."[97] Committee meetings were held five times a year with branch store executives and covered topics ranging from personnel to advertising, merchandise and credit and customer complaints. At the officer level, the position of director of planning and development was created in 1962 to oversee branch expansion across the Delaware Valley.

It was in this growth-minded decade that company officers made the decision to refer to all employees, no matter what their position, division or department, as "Associates." As the company became more complex, it remained important that everyone felt they were part of the family. This ethos would later be underscored in the company's 1987 employee handbook, which said that "in business, Associates work together to accomplish common goals."

As S&C entered the 1970s, the drive to be the Delaware Valley's dominant retailer was paramount. It was just a few years earlier, in 1967, that Stockton had announced, "The future holds no limits to our company's expansion. We are striving for dominance in the eight-county Delaware Valley area.... We hope to be able to grow at the rate of one new unit every two years."[98]

CLOVER

Expansion, however, was not to be confused with recklessness. "Do not hasten to change good habits and customs for the sake of doing something different": these were the cautionary words of Isaac H. Clothier Jr. at a Quarter Century Club annual banquet.[99] Stockton shared this sentiment and expressed it to the company officers during a meeting to brainstorm the expansion policy for the 1970s. He emphasized, "Don't get carried away with the lure of untapped but distant markets until we have firmly entrenched ourselves in those close to home."[100] Stockton had been closely watching the path of S&C's competitors and saw the stumbles they took as they expanded too quickly: the costs associated with more distant locations, the logistical barriers of supplying and operating far-away branches and how such branches distract from the business of branch stores closer to home. These costs forced local retailers to hand over control to outside investors. Gimbels was acquired by a conglomerate in 1973, and Lit Brothers closed all its stores in 1977. In 1978, the Wanamaker family sold its ownership to Carter Hawley Hale, the largest department store chain in the west.

S&C's goal was to expand, but regionally, and to do so in a calculated and measured way. One calculation proposed by Stockton was to enter the

Warren White didn't know exactly why Stockton was so reluctant to use the term *discount*. "He just didn't want to put the name S&C in the same sentence as 'discount,'" he said.*

_____

* Warren White, in discission with the author, January 2022.

discount store market—or "mass merchandise," as he and other officers preferred to call it. Discount merchandising emerged in the 1950s and had tripled in business by the 1970s. Stores like Target, Kmart and Ayr-Way appealed to the young, working- and middle-class families who were moving to the suburbs—as S&C officer Frank Veale described them, "the kind of people Sears and Penny's and Woolworths have been serving so successfully for years."[101] The discount business was clearly growing at a faster rate than department stores, but fortunately for S&C, the market had not yet been saturated in the Delaware Valley. Always trying to stay ahead of the competition, S&C, under the leadership of Stockton, decided the timing was right.

"It was a very smart decision," said Warren White, who became the general manager for the Clover division. "People were moving out to the suburbs in great quantity, and that's where the business was. They didn't want to park and take the train or have things delivered to their house two or three days after they bought it. They wanted it now."[102]

On November 12, 1969, the S&C board approved the decision to name its new venture Clover, in honor of S&C's popular Clover Day sales. Clover Days were unique to the region, and the name Clover had become synonymous with savings and value. Peter Strawbridge, Stockton's eldest son, was chosen to lead the way as general manager. He had put in eight years with the company as a department manager and branch store manager. Although Clover would be considered a division of S&C, it would operate "as a distinct and separate entity with no direct relationship to the traditional department store operations of the parent company."[103] It had its own corporate offices, initially located at Fourth and Walnut Streets in Philadelphia and later moved to Eighth and Market in order to save on expenses. Along with fashion and apparel for the entire family, the store would sell notions, over-the-counter drugs, garden supplies, auto supplies and sporting goods and contain a food market.

On February 25, 1971, S&C's first Clover store opened in Marlton, New Jersey, and in September, the second Clover store opened in Blackwood, New Jersey. Concerns hung in the air over whether these new stores would detract from S&C's business of running its branch stores and whether the

Exterior of Marlton Clover Store

First Clover store in Marlton, New Jersey, February 1971. *Courtesy of the author.*

public would approve of this new look for the company. Concerns soon subsided as shoppers showed up in droves for the grand openings.

The first three years were not without challenges, however. Burlington Coat Factory, Kings and Kmart were already doing business in the region. Furthermore, there were considerable learning curves, which Peter Strawbridge acknowledged in the book *Family Business: The Momentous Seventies.* "We went into the Clover business with insufficient information and unrealistic expectations for too much too soon."[104] Staff came from a department store background and were inexperienced in discount stores. They incorrectly expected the Clover division to have the same success rate as the department store division. There was also a lack of "constant and aggressive promotion with consistently focused advertising."[105] After Clover corrected for these mistakes, it was clear by 1974 that the division was a success. The annual report for 1975 noted that earnings for the company as a whole increased 46.3 percent over 1974.

By the mid-seventies, the company discarded the euphemism *mass merchandise* and embraced the term *discount* but with the resolve to be a superior discount store. Again, the company set itself apart from its competitors by highlighting its main asset, its employees. Clover employees (or Associates, as they were referred to, like their S&C counterparts) would provide the same stellar customer service found in S&C branch stores. Warren White recalled that early on, many Clover Associates were brought over from S&C. "They of course knew the atmosphere and they brought that atmosphere with them." As the Clover division grew, he credits its

Clover store checkout lines, 1970s. *Courtesy of the Hagley Museum and Library.*

Personnel Department with being "very careful with who they hired. Just as careful as S&C was." Warren often wrote letters to employees who received commendations from customers, congratulating them on the positive feedback and reminding them how much they were appreciated. "We just stood apart miles in customer service," said Warren.[106]

Former Clover Associate Pete O'Grady might say they stood miles apart in employee culture as well. Pete worked as an auditor for Clover in the mid-1980s. Once, when visiting Texas, he toured his first Target store. "Target was much more of a machine. It seemed really disciplined, everyone was in uniforms, khakis and red shirts. I remember thinking it was very organized but more like an army. Clover was a family."[107]

Over the next two decades, the company would open twenty-four more Clover stores and become the dominant discount retailer in the region, holding that title until 1996. It joined the International Mass Retail Association (IMRA), the trade association for discount stores, which consisted of some of the oldest names in discounting, including Walmart, Kmart and Target. In 1991, Warren White was elected chairman of the

IMRA's board of directors, and in 1993, the IMRA recognized his years of excellent leadership by honoring him with three different awards at its national convention.[108]

Warren White: "I Was Being Interviewed All Along"

Warren White. *Courtesy of the author.*

Warren White had just received his master's degree in retailing from the University of Pittsburgh when he, along with two other graduates, was recruited by S&C in 1957.

Warren would spend his early years with the company as an assistant buyer in the Domestic Floor Covering Department, where he learned not just about carpets and rugs but also about "customers and how to satisfy them." After proving himself in Domestic Floor Coverings and being promoted to buyer, he was asked in 1968 to become the divisional merchandise manager of the company's Budget Store. S&C had a total of three Budget Stores, including the one at Eighth and Market, which was in the basement of the large building. Customers could find new merchandise sold at a lower price scale in the Budget Stores. (Once Clover opened, S&C kept open the Budget Store located at Eighth and Market and closed the other two.) Admittedly, Warren knew nothing about this type of merchandise, so he hit the ground running, absorbing as much as he could and building a whole new skill set.

Just two years later, Warren was the first person hired onto the new Clover division's management team. As general merchandise manager, he worked closely with Peter Strawbridge, again hitting the ground running and learning as much as he could about this new business. He clearly made his mark; Clover would be his home for the remainder of his career. In 1979, he became general manager (replacing Peter Strawbridge, who became president of S&C), and in 1981, he joined the board of directors.

After more than sixty years since he first arrived at S&C as a young graduate, Warren has had time to reflect and wonder if his fate hadn't been a little premeditated. He recalled some peculiar visits dating back to his time as assistant buyer in Carpets. In those days, the assistant buyer was required to work the store's full hours, which meant he had to stay late two days a week when the store had its extended evening hours. Curiously, to him, S&C's president, Randall Copeland, began visiting him on those evenings. The two would talk about the business: what was working, what wasn't. "I always thought it was strange that the president of the company would come in and talk to an assistant buyer at night." These visits continued when he moved into the Budget Store, until one day, after just over ten years of being with S&C, he received a phone call from Peter Strawbridge with the invitation to join him in leading the company's new venture.

When thinking about his earlier recruitment from the University of Pittsburgh, Warren muses, "S&C went to that school and picked up three people to see if there was anybody there that might be able to get them into the boom discount business." That much is clear to him.

Whether or not his musings are correct, it's obvious S&C chose wisely in hiring someone who was up for the challenge of taking on and excelling at every task he was given. "I was there from the beginning of Clover to the end. It was a fantastic career."[109]

CHAPTER 5

FOOD, GLORIOUS FOOD!

You would go in and there was nice pretty carpeting. Oh, it was big.
The Corinthian Room was big! We took pride in the dining room,
keeping it nice and clean.
—Pat Foltz Martino, Corinthian Room waitress, 1977–87

DINING SERVICES

By the late nineteenth century, many department stores had figured out the importance of offering food services to their customers, who needed a place to rest their weary feet and refuel before continuing with their shopping. By 1904, S&C had expanded into a five-story cube on Market Street with twelve acres of floor space. On the top floor was a restaurant divided into two sections. Alfred Lief describes how one section was for mixed company, so smoking was not permitted, while the other was for men who lit cigars and lady companions who did not object.[110] Over time, department stores invested in large, stately dining rooms designed to make customers feel catered to and indulged. John Wanamaker's had the Crystal Tea Room, Lit Brothers had the Jefferson Room and by 1932, S&C was welcoming the public to dine in its grand, sixth-floor Corinthian Dining Room. An ambiance of class was created with white table linens, uniformed waitstaff and floor-to-ceiling arched windows that let the sun's rays greet shoppers. It wasn't just customers who dined in the Corinthian Room. S&C employees

Corinthian Dining Room at Eighth and Market Street store. *Courtesy of the Hagley Museum and Library.*

enjoyed treating their friends and family to lunch when they were in town. Company officers regularly took their lunch in the Pickwick Room, a smaller dining area that sat at the south end of the main dining room and better accommodated their business discussions.

As the store expanded into surrounding suburbs and towns, each branch had a restaurant with its own distinct style and menu. The Cherry Hill store was known for its Italian cuisine, "The Aquarium" at Willow Grove featured fresh fish and kept diners entertained with an eight-hundred-gallon saltwater tank stocked with tropical fish and a shark and Christiana had the Chesapeake Room with a stone fireplace displayed in the center to provide a warm atmosphere. However, none was as grand as the Corinthian Room. In truth, providing dining services was a huge expense for the store. Operating costs increased in the 1980s and 1990s as competition grew from fast food alternatives in shopping malls. Yet even as many department stores, including S&C, began to cut back on dining services, the company insisted on keeping the Corinthian Room intact with its linens and table service. One attempt at boosting restaurant sales came in the late 1970s, when the decision was made to finally permit the sale of alcohol in all store restaurants so shoppers could imbibe while they ate. The holdout was due to the founders' Quaker adherence to temperance, which extended to the store's advertising. The word *cocktail* was forbidden to be used in ads. In his book *Family Business: Strawbridge & Clothier: The Momentous Seventies*, Frank Veale highlights the policy change with sarcasm when he remarks that cocktails "do not signify the moral collapse of S&C. It is still the policy of the company to oppose sin."[111] Alternatively, smoking was permitted in ads, as long as it was a man smoking. Women could not be shown smoking until the 1940s.

CORINTHIAN DINING ROOM MEMORIES

Donna Elman Fine
Corinthian Room Waitress, 1962–66

"I looked like a French maid. I wore my hair up in a bun, and that was covered in a net. A black, shiny, short-sleeved A-line skirt. I had to kneel on the floor, and the hem of my skirt had to hit the floor. I had to wear pantyhose and sensible shoes. I had a little white apron with a little pocket."

Donna remembers waiting on Justus's son Francis R. Strawbridge, or "old man Strawbridge," as she referred to him. He used to tip her a quarter. She made eighty-six cents an hour, and you didn't have to declare tips at that time, so a quarter wasn't bad. "I think he shined his money. He had a black purse that clipped together, like a woman's." He would take it out, open it up, take out a shiny quarter and hand it to her. He never left it on the table.

"It was like another family. I loved the waitresses; I was the only college kid. Some had worked there a long time: twenty, thirty years. Most were Catholic; I'm Jewish. They would light candles for me every time I had finals. They were sweet and supportive."[112]

6TH FLOOR WAITRESSES—L. to r.: Hilda Gallagher, Adele Connor, Ida Flanagan, Doris Horn, Viola Fraunfelter, Martha Biester, Marion Roe (see photo, next page, for others).

Corinthian Dining Room waitstaff, 1963. *Courtesy of the Hagley Museum and Library.*

Pat Foltz Martino
Corinthian Room Waitress, 1977–87

Pat Foltz Martino remembers fellow waitress Hilda, who had worked in the Corinthian Room for fifty years. "She really didn't want to leave. The supervisor at the time found a way to keep her. She had one or two small tables, by the kitchen. I think she had a couple of customers who came in just for her."[113]

Ron Dipinto
Director of Food Services

Ron DiPinto. *Courtesy of Ron DiPinto.*

Ron Dipinto worked at S&C for nearly thirteen years before finding himself in charge of food services in 1983. Initially on the merchandise track after completing the Executive Development Program, he eventually switched to operations and did everything from being major appliances service manager to furniture complaint manager to human resources manager for the Springfield, Echelon and Jenkintown branch stores. "They sent me all over the place. I felt like I was a troubleshooter for the store," recalled Ron. When the director of food services position became vacant, it was clear that Ron's capable people and managerial skills were a perfect fit for the demands of the job. Yet when offered the position, his response was, "I know nothing about food other than I eat it." He was assured that being a good administrator was enough. Reluctant, he said he'd do it for three years. Fourteen years later, when the company was sold, he was still in charge of food.

Ron recalled hitting the ground running on his first day. "I walked into the office and got a call from Stockton. 'What are the soups today?' I said, 'I don't know.' 'You are the food director, aren't you? I would suggest you know the soups every day.'" Not only did Ron learn the soup of the day at the Corinthian Room, but he also took charge of the entire menu as well as the menus for all the branch store restaurants. Along with the restaurants, Ron oversaw the employee cafeterias and managed numerous special events like the Quarter Century Club banquets, board of director meetings and celebrity visits. He also played a role in S&C's Food Hall in the 1980s and 1990s, overseeing product production. Under Ron's direction, thousands of S&C customers and employees were served daily.

He admits that he stayed on as director of food services, as well as with the company, longer than he expected because he knew everybody. "I was good friends with a lot of people. It was an experience I would never want to give up."[114]

THE FOOD HALL

In 1982, S&C turned its attention to the emerging market of gourmet food and developed the Food Hall. Stockton's eldest son, Peter Strawbridge, who became president of the company in 1979 (Stockton transitioned to chairman of the board's executive committee), was the vision behind this new venture. It was part of S&C's continuous quest to heighten the customer experience, set itself apart from its competitors and keep its Center City store vibrant. S&C was no stranger to food merchandise. It had long been lauded for running the largest candy business in the city, thanks to its relationship with local candymaker Chester A. Asher Inc. It also sold packaged coffee beans and leased space on the first floor to Hanscom's bakery, which, in addition to baked goods, sold prepackaged entrées. Peter's idea would not only significantly expand the company's selection of food merchandise, but it would also create an entirely new experience for S&C customers. Inspired by the food hall at Harrods Department store in London, Peter wanted to bring that old-world charm to Philadelphia. He also wanted to figure out the best use for the store's isolated and increasingly less frequented Notions Department, which occupied a whopping 8,500 square feet in the far west corner on the ground floor. It was a big risk—but per the S&C way, a very calculated one. Food culture in the United States came alive in the 1980s.

More and more boutique restaurants were opening in cities like Philadelphia. TV was airing more cooking shows with popular new chefs, and Americans were taking more interest in different types of cuisine. According to Robert Cressy, the Food Hall's first director, Peter was "very much on the trend."[115]

On November 15, 1982, S&C shoppers entered a world of "fine foods." Robert Cressy objected to the word *gourmet*, which he said implies "pricey." "Fine food does not have to be pricey," he explained in a 1983 interview with *Philadelphia Magazine*. Cressy worked with Ben Thompson, the architect behind Boston's Faneuil Hall Marketplace and Baltimore's Harborplace, on the design. He wanted to avoid what he described as the rigidity many department stores had and how "they lose the sense of communication of a neighborhood store."[116] The result was a neighborhood setting with separate small shops that included local Philadelphia ice-cream maker Bassets, a café located on the mezzanine level, Bread & Co. bakery along with Hanscom's bakery and a deli shop that sold sliced meats, gourmet cheeses, fresh pasta and takeout salads. Cooking demonstrations and recipe giveaways were frequent attractions. There were also special monthly themes. The Food Hall strove to create a welcoming atmosphere rather than an intimidating one. Shoppers could grab a light lunch or coffee and sit and enjoy the marketplace ambiance—and so could S&C employees.

Robert Cressy
Food Hall Director

Robert (Bob) Cressy came to S&C when he was eighteen seeking part-time employment during the holiday season. He quickly discovered his love for retail and took a full-time position, eventually becoming the S&C buyer for china. One day several years into his career, Peter Strawbridge called him into his office. Bob said he felt like he was being called to the principal's office, since it wasn't every day that the president of the company asked to speak with him. When Bob was seated in his tenth-floor office, Peter proceeded to outline his vision of putting a European-style food operation on the first floor of the Eighth and Market store and said he would like Bob to make it happen. Peter said he had heard that Bob enjoyed cooking and entertaining and that he had the personality to make

Robert Cressy.
Courtesy of Robert Cressy.

this vision come true. Stunned, Bob thought, "I'm the china buyer; I don't know anything about the food business!" He kept this to himself, however, not wanting to say no to the president. The next thing he knew, he was on an airplane to Boston to meet with Ben Thompson, the acclaimed architect for the project. From that point on, Bob's life revolved around this massive undertaking: hiring and training employees, working with vendors and suppliers and, most importantly, getting the word out about S&C's new venture and speaking with the press.

Any concerns and doubts about the Food Hall's success quickly vanished on opening day. Bob remembers the place being packed with people. Every local news station was present to capture the moment. He spent the day giving interviews in between managing opening day logistics. It was two o'clock in the morning before he finally went home after dealing with a broken dishwasher and making sure they had enough food for the next day, since they had run out. "Every day up to Christmas, the place was cheek by jowl," Bob said.

Despite the demanding hours and pressures of the job, Bob loved the immediate gratification of managing the Food Hall. Conversely, he admitted that one of the challenges of the job was immediate dissatisfaction. "If you came up in the middle of the night with an idea for a new salad and [went] to the kitchen in the morning and [said], 'Let's try this,' by noon you'd be putting it in the case; by 3:00 p.m., you'd know whether it was a winner or loser."

In addition to being popular among shoppers, the Food Hall was a hit with employees. In Bob's opinion, the advantage it had over other food markets in the city, like the Reading Terminal Market, was that it was located in a building with over three thousand employees, most of whom had to enter the Food Hall when they arrived to work. They couldn't escape the "aroma centers" that were scattered around the market: the freshly roasted coffee, the morning muffins or the bacon that was used for lunchtime sandwiches. Employees were as much an important customer base as the public.

Bob's favorite time while at the Food Hall was his first holiday season. He enjoyed coming up with "special things that set us apart from every other food operation in and around the city"—like the three-pound box of chocolate that he asked Asher Candy to make and package in a red S&C box, which local salesmen bought in droves to give to their clients.

Overall, Bob stressed that the success of the Food Hall was a collaborative effort involving every vendor and salesperson. He gave special acknowledgement to Wesley Craig the candy buyer, "whose knowledge of that industry was invaluable." The deli and café would not have run smoothly without Jan Torisian, and the Food Hall would not have received as much press coverage without Sylvia Kay, who was responsible for special events and PR, bringing in such stars as Julia Child and the Galloping Gourmet.

After three incredibly demanding years as director of the Food Hall, Bob told Peter he "needed to get his life back." He turned the job over to Jan Torisian and became the buyer for Decorative Housewares, which allowed him to pursue his passion for Christmas trim. In 1995, he took a job with the AMC as head of its holiday division. Looking back, Bob said, "The store was very good to me. It taught me a lot. On top of it, there were wonderful people who worked there. I never felt my work was a drudge....Retail is an exciting business. You never have an idle moment. And there's something about the buzz of a department store."[117]

FOOD HALL MEMORIES

Gina Major
Public Relations and Special Events Manager, 1980–84

"Oh my gosh, the food was incredible! I'm quite positive that all the employees would eat there." When Gina came to work each morning, she entered through the back door, which brought her right to the Food Hall. That experience has not left her memory. "The sight, the first smell in the morning, Food Hall muffins and Food Hall coffee. So strong, so recurring, so unique and fabulous. It is just embedded in my senses."[118]

Wesley Craig
Candy and Gourmet Foods Buyer, 1970–96

The Food Hall was an immediate success. The candy business doubled overnight, the existing packaged gourmet foods volume grew by 50 percent and the whole-bean coffee business equaled the packaged gourmet food volume in the first year! The fresh cheese and deli counter also enjoyed great success. The small restaurant that was built out from the existing office mezzanine was jammed every day for lunch.

The swarm of people on opening day was a pleasant surprise for all of us. It looked like a November Clover Day in the Food Hall! By 2:00 p.m., I had to climb a stock ladder and refill at least half of the coffee bean containers because we had sold so much coffee that day. This meant dumping coffee beans from thirty-pound bags into the top of these containers.

The study, design and highly successful operation of the S&C Food Hall stand out as one of the most rewarding times I spent in my twenty-five years at S&C! There is no doubt it helped us consolidate ourselves as a destination store.[119]

CHAPTER 6

ALL IN THE FAMILY

As part of our Store Family, you will quickly discover an atmosphere of friendliness and enthusiasm throughout our stores. All of our Associates have achieved this for us and we hope you will want to continue this tradition.
—S&C employee handbook, 1987

P eople are our most priceless asset." These words were spoken by Justus Strawbridge's grandson Stockton in 1971, but the sentiment dates to the company's founding in 1868. It was important to Justus and Isaac to create a company that not just employed people but also provided an environment where they could pursue their interests, hone skills, excel and build a secure career with the company. Their success was the company's success and vice versa. The following pages show how the company incorporated these objectives and values into its operations.

EMPLOYEE BENEFITS

Before S&C's employer-based health insurance and benefits packages, benefits programs were initiated and managed by employees. S&C officers encouraged and financially supported these initiatives. The physical health and well-being of employees were as important as job training.

Relief Association ad, 1911 *Store Chat. Courtesy of the author.*

In 1880, S&C employees formed the Relief Association, one of the first such organizations in the retail industry. Organized and controlled by employees, the Association provided a safety net for those who fell ill. There was a fifty-cent initiation fee. Benefits paid to eligible members were five dollars a week for up to fifteen weeks each year, with a one-hundred-dollar death benefit. Assessments were only paid if the treasury fell below one hundred dollars, in which case, the assessment was twenty-five cents a month. S&C showed its support for the association by covering the costs of any late payment fines or other rules infractions.[120]

In 1884, employees formed the S&C Savings Fund Association. Members paid between twenty-five cents and five dollars per week for shares. After fifty-two weeks, they withdrew what was standing to their credit. Isaac Clothier enthusiastically supported the employee-led initiative. He was a firm believer in the practice of saving and that it would make for not just better employees but also better citizens. The company agreed to serve as custodian of the funds and pay 6 percent interest.[121]

In 1907, employees yet again organized, this time to start a pension fund. According to an April 1907 article in *Store Chat*, "So far as the Store Chat knows, this is the first large store to move for a pension fund to be organized and governed by its employees, and we believe it will be the forerunner of others throughout the country." Members paid monthly dues of $0.15 and began making payouts when the fund reached $50,000. After only three years, this goal was reached, thanks in part to a $7,400 investment by the company and fundraising events organized by employee organizations such as the S&C Orchestra and baseball team. Funds were also raised by the store's Minstrel Show Association, which held performances around the store (an unpleasant reminder of the racism that was prevalent and unquestioned at the time).[122]

Starting in the 1930s, new federal welfare programs were created, and companies began to assume the management and operation of employee benefits. With the introduction of Social Security, S&C took over the obligations of the pension fund so that it could supplement Social Security payments to employees. In 1953, the Relief Association ended, and the company introduced its Welfare Benefit plan, which covered sickness, accidents, hospitalization and life insurance. In 1957, the company was the first department store in Philadelphia to establish a contract with the Associated Hospital Service of Philadelphia (later known as Independence Blue Cross) for employee hospitalization and medical insurance.[123]

Throughout the next four decades, S&C prided itself on providing its employees with healthy benefits packages. *Store Chat* routinely publicized the amount the company paid toward benefits. It reported in 1989 that for the nearly fifteen thousand Associates in the department store and Clover divisions, a total of $45,661,994 was paid in personnel benefits.[124] Market changes in the 1990s led to a reduction in benefits.

HEALTH AND FITNESS

In 1910, S&C purchased a vacant lot the size of one city block at Sixty-Second, Walnut and Locust Streets. It was Herbert Tily's suggestion that the field be used for athletic activities, which led to the formation of the S&C Athletic Association. Isaac Clothier supported the idea, believing in the "necessity of outdoor exercise for those who worked indoors."[125] The company opened the field in July that year with a baseball game between executives and buyers. "Spectators and participants numbered 3,000."[126] In addition to baseball, a lawn tennis committee was formed to organize matches. The field was frequently used for special store-sponsored events such as the Memorial Day Meet, a daylong track and field event for employees, and an annual Summer Fete. S&C's youngest employees also benefitted from the athletic association and fields. Junior sports leagues were organized, and the company held an annual children's outing, a day of friendly competition followed by a dinner and dance. In 1911, an indoor gymnasium was installed at S&C's newly purchased garage located on the southeast corner of the athletic field. It was equipped with men's and women's lockers, dressing rooms and showers. S&C employees could join winter sports leagues for basketball, indoor tennis and volleyball and enjoy an "impromptu dance" after games every Monday night.[127] Bowling was another popular sport among employees.

Sadly, many of the sports leagues had to disband when the athletic field was sold in 1926. Four years after becoming a corporation, the company was facing rising costs and the need to answer to stockholders. It feared becoming vulnerable to potential takeover bids should it not maintain its financial health. This prompted it to sell off some of its "slow assets."[128] Fortunately for many employees, the bowling, softball and basketball leagues remained intact until 1996, playing at different public parks and centers.

Top: S&C athletic fields, 1910. *Courtesy of the Hagley Museum and Library.*

Middle: Relay races at the annual children's outing, 1912. *Courtesy of the author.*

Right: Young girl participant in the annual children's outing, 1911. *Courtesy of the author.*

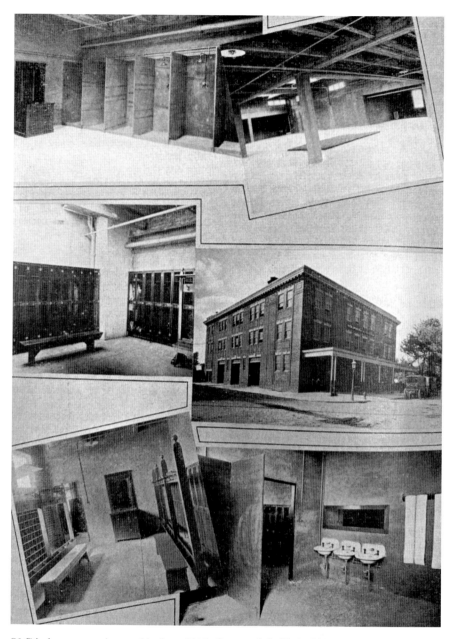

S&C indoor gymnasium and lockers, 1911. *Courtesy of the Hagley Museum and Library.*

Delivery Department Basket Ball Team

Top: Delivery Department basketball team, early 1900s. *Courtesy of the Hagley Museum and Library.*

Bottom: Women's basketball team, 1910. *Courtesy of the author.*

S&C baseball team, early 1900s. *Courtesy of the Hagley Museum and Library.*

S&C softball team, 1987. *Courtesy of the author.*

S&C bowling team member, 1960s. *Courtesy of the author.*

During Debbie Herron Jeffreys's first week at S&C as an assistant buyer in women's shoes in 1983, she was invited to an S&C softball game by fellow employees. New and not knowing anyone, she initially hesitated but finally agreed after some encouragement. Looking back, she's glad she did. "I had one of the best times. This was a huge thing. Everybody went. It was a must do social event!"[129]

The company also invested in a seashore cottage in 1910, where women and young girl employees could spend their vacation time in the fresh ocean air enjoying plenty of exercise. The cabin was located in North Wildwood, New Jersey, and women paid three dollars a week to board and take their meals. Men and young boys could spend their vacation time at a YMCA camp in the Jersey Pines for a discounted rate. This perk likely also ended in the 1920s. A more modern take on company-organized vacations emerged in the 1960s when the Personnel Department created the S&C Recreational Association. Trips were organized for employees to several destinations both near and far, including the Poconos, quaint New England towns, national parks and European locations.

To provide for the medical needs of its employees, the company established an on-site medical room at Eighth and Market in 1898.[130] The physician was Dr. Rachel R. Williams, a recent graduate of the Women's Medical College and the sister-in-law of Justus's son Edward Strawbridge. Dr. Williams held consultations with employees once a week in her small office tucked away in a corner on the furniture floor. By 1910, Dr. Williams's office had moved to a different part of the store and was referred to as "hospital quarters." After World War I, she provided full-time service and had a nurse on staff to assist her. She also contracted with a dentist to begin providing dental services to employees who paid twenty-five cents an extraction.[131] In 1948, at the age of eighty-two, Dr. Williams was recognized for fifty years of service to S&C; she retired shortly thereafter.[132] After her passing in 1962 at the age of ninety-five, the company continued providing on-site medical care. A nurse's office was open for visits from nine to five o'clock on the eleventh floor and provided beds for sick employees. A nurse's station was also provided in each of the branch stores.

S&C beach house, Wildwood, New Jersey, 1910. *Courtesy of the Hagley Museum and Library.*

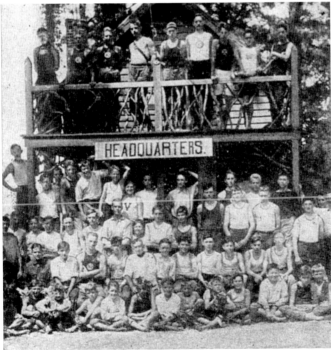

Above: S&C young women enjoying time at the beach, 1911. *Courtesy of the author.*

Left: S&C young men at Camp Kenilworth, 1913. *Courtesy of the Hagley Museum and Library.*

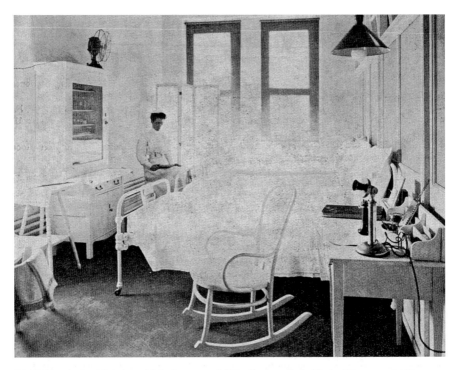

S&C's hospital at Eighth and Market store, 1909. *Courtesy of the Hagley Museum and Library.*

Dr. Rachel R. Williams is recognized for fifty years of service. *Courtesy of the Hagley Museum and Library.*

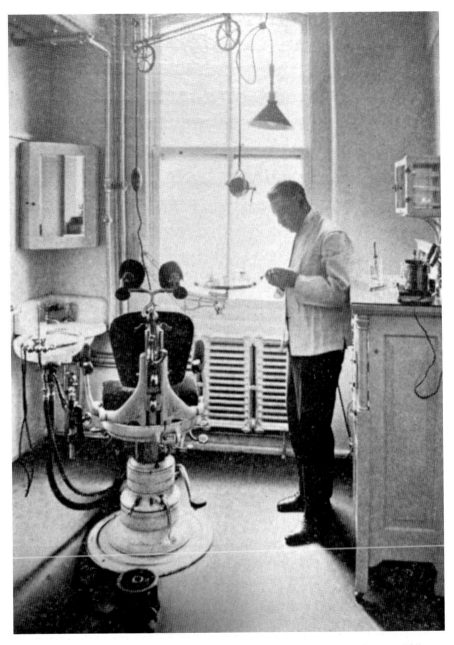

S&C's dental room at Eighth and Market store, 1911. *Courtesy of the Hagley Museum and Library.*

Susan Kearney remembers when she first learned about the nurse's office at the Eighth and Market store where she worked as a part-time sales associate from 1975 to 1982. It was the Saturday before Easter, and she confided to another sales associate that she wasn't feeling well. The sales associate, an older lady who had worked at S&C for several decades, told Susan to go upstairs to the nurse. Surprised by this information, Susan went upstairs, and sure enough, there was a nurse dressed all in uniform. She expected the nurse would give her an aspirin and send her on her way, but instead, she was invited to lie down on one of the three hospital beds located in a separate room. After resting, Susan returned to the third floor and told her colleague, "They have a whole hospital up there!"[133]

Employees could become trained as S&C First Aiders, ready to administer first aid to customers and store Associates alike. A 1984 *Store Chat* article reported that First Aiders responded to over 770 customer and employee accidents that year.

CREATURE COMFORTS

For a store to be really successful, improved working conditions and greater benefits for its employees must go hand in hand with improved facilities and service for its customers.
—*Dwight Perkins, president 1947–55, chairman of the board 1955–67*

Early on there were not many comforts…no employee rest rooms or customer waiting rooms, heated with hot air gas lights. On one occasion it was so cold the gas pipes froze and our only lights were lanterns here and there on the counters…no fine dining, with a cafeteria at which food could be furnished at little cost.…Each year has added to our pleasure and our convenience.
—*Martha Dogherty,* Store Chat, *June 15, 1918*

It did not take long for the company to understand the importance of creating a comfortable shopping and working environment. Lounges and cafeterias were needed not just for customers but also for the people who kept customers coming back. One of the expansions of the Eighth and Market store in the early 1900s included an inviting outdoor lounge area on its roof for female employees (who made up the majority of salespeople).

Women employees enjoying the rooftop lounge, early 1900s. *Courtesy of the Hagley Museum and Library.*

They could rest their legs from standing and stretch out on steamer chairs for twenty-five-minute breaks in the morning and afternoon. Employee lounges would become standard features with the new Eighth and Market store in 1932 and future branch stores.

The early 1900s also saw the introduction of employee cafeterias. Previously, employees would find their own place to take their lunch. George Stevens, who started his decades-long career with S&C in 1876, fondly recounted that "everybody brought their lunch, and it was at this midday feast, sitting on a case or a bolt of cotton flannel, we all had a merry time discussing the topics of the Store."[134]

An employee cafeteria must have been installed some time before 1907, based on a *Store Chat* article from that year that reads, "The employee dining room is an interesting place at all times, but especially is this true of it at the witching hour of twelve, when girls, young and old, big and little, blonde and brunette, are congregating from all sides at this lunch-time Mecca of women employees." Whether the male employees ate at a separate time is not mentioned.

Decades later, the waitstaff in the Corinthian Room took their meals in the kitchen, enjoying the same menu items as the customers.

> *When the restaurant closed at the end of the day, we could eat in the back after our shift. We could have a full meal and dessert. They fed us really, really well….We could eat anything on the menu for free unless it was steak.*
> —Donna Elman Fine, Corinthian Room waitress 1962–66 [135]

EIGHTH AND MARKET

Every branch was a community unto itself. Eighth and Market was a city
unto itself. It had an energy all its own.
—*Debbie Herron Jeffreys, merchandise information trainer 1983–87* [136]

The Eighth and Market store was the hub of activity throughout the life of
the company. Referred to by employees as the Main Store, the Flagship or
Headquarters, it was home to offices for S&C and Clover's top executives,
the board of directors' boardroom and many of the company's operations,
such as the advertising, human resources and finance departments. It also
housed a wide variety of public amenities between the 1930s and 1990s,
such as a pharmacy, a post office, a travel agency, a repair center, an optical
and hearing aid center, a portrait studio, gift wrap services, a wig salon, a
belowground subway entrance and, later, the Food Hall.

If I had a gynecologist in the building, I would never have to leave.
—*Dorette Rota Jackson, S&C* Store Chat *editor 1987–96* [137]

The aesthetic and design of the building also set it apart. No other branch
store looked like the Eighth and Market store with its pyramid design and
setbacks. And no other branch store had the same interior attractions enjoyed
by employees and customers. The most noteworthy being Il Porcellino,
the Wild Boar, a four-thousand-pound bronze sculpture and fountain that
greeted shoppers in the first-floor elevator lobby.
The fountain became a store landmark in 1966.
Executives had traveled to the Straw Market of
Florence, Italy, in preparation for the storewide
Italian festival, which showcased Italian culture
and merchandise. When their eyes fell on the Il
Porcellino sculpture at the market, they knew they
had to commission a replica for the festival. From
then on, the boar endeared itself to shoppers and
employees alike, who would pause to rub its snout
for good luck, drop coins into the fountain pool,
take a minute to rest on the large black marble
base Il Porcellino sat on or use the landmark as a
popular meeting spot. Wanamaker's had its eagle,
and Strawbridge & Clothier had its boar.

Hundreds of dollars in
coins were collected from
the fountain pool each year
and donated by S&C to the
United Way.*

A second Il Porcellino
was made for S&C's King
of Prussia branch store,
which opened in 1988.

---

* *Store Chat* 77, no. 1 (January–
February 1986): 3.

This model of the Seal of Confidence was fired as a ceramic tile mosaic to adorn the rear wall of the Eighth and Market store elevators, installed when they were automated. *Courtesy of the author.*

Architect's rendering of the new S&C building at Eighth and Market Streets. *Courtesy of the Hagley Museum and Library.*

Right: The Eighth
and Market Streets
flagship S&C store.
Courtesy of the author.

Below: Sketch of
the Whiteland
Clover store,
the first to open
with automated
checkout counters
and scanners,
October 19, 1988.
Courtesy of the author.

Top: A cash register that was used in the early years of Strawbridge & Clothier. It stood in a case at the entrance to the S&C History Gallery and served as a "symbol of our business." *Courtesy of the author.*

Bottom: A selection of S&C shopping bags. *Courtesy of the author.*

Above: S&C Blue Credit Card. *Courtesy of Betsy Horen.*

Left: Il Porcellino, elevator lobby at Eighth and Market store, 1970s. *Courtesy of the author.*

Ground floor of the Eighth and Market store, 1990s. *Courtesy of the author.*

Information booth at the Eighth and Market store, 1970s. *Courtesy of the author.*

Top: Entrance to the Food Hall. *Courtesy of the author.*

Bottom: Food Hall mezzanine, 1980s. *Courtesy of the author.*

Store Chat cover depicting Quarter Century Club logo. *Courtesy of the Hagley Museum and Library.*

Left: Food Hall deli counters and displays, 1980s. *Courtesy of the author.*

Below: A Christmas wreath adorns the entrance to the Eighth and Market store, 1980s. *Courtesy of the author.*

This page and opposite: Store Chat holiday covers. *Courtesy of the author.*

Strawbridge & Clothier   Nov.-Dec. 1985

STORE CHAT

A DICKENS CHRISTMAS

S&C catalogue holiday cover. Roy Miller, graphic designer and illustrator in the Advertising Department from 1968 to 1996, was proud to have his illustration grace the cover of S&C's Christmas catalogue in 1974. The catalogue was mailed to thousands of Delaware Valley residents. Roy was the first person of color to illustrate the catalogue's cover. *Courtesy of Roy Miller.*

A scene from S&C's "A Christmas Carol" display, 1985. *Courtesy of the author.*

The fourth and fifth generation. *Left to right, seated*: Jennifer Gorman-Strawbridge, David W. Strawbridge, Steven L. Strawbridge, Steven L. Strawbridge Jr. *Left to right, standing*: Peter S. Strawbridge, G. Stockton Strawbridge, Francis R. Strawbridge III, Isaac H. Clothier IV. *Courtesy of the author.*

When our doors first opened on the corner of 8th and Market Streets in 1868, we had no idea that we would grow to become Philadelphia's Family Business and make millions of friends.

So now, in closing our doors for the last time and turning over the business to new owners, we look back with pride and fond memories. And we wish to express our deepest gratitude.

Thank you
to our customers for your patronage, your support and, most importantly, your friendship. Serving you has been a pleasure.

Thank you
to every member of our Store Family, past and present. As times and trends have changed, your dedication and commitment to excellence have remained constant. You have always been our greatest strength— working with you has been an honor.

THANK YOU

PHILADELPHIA AND THE ENTIRE DELAWARE VALLEY

FOR 128 WONDERFUL YEARS!

strawbridge & clothier

Farewell ad in the *Philadelphia Inquirer. Courtesy of the author.*

Store Chat remembers...

who we were, what we've done and where we've been together.

Above: Cover of the last *Store Chat*, July 1996. *Courtesy of the author.*

Left: Unveiling ceremony for the S&C historical marker that stands in front of the former flagship store at Eighth and Market Streets. *Courtesy of Mike Dougherty, South Jersey reporter, KYW Newsradio 103.9 FM.*

The Il Porcellino fountain in the old S&C elevator lobby at Eighth and Market, which now serves as a lounge for customers of the GIANT Heirloom Market. *Courtesy of the GIANT Company.*

S&C's gold chandeliers hang above fresh produce in the GIANT Heirloom Market. *Courtesy of the GIANT Company.*

Other interior attractions included the large murals by American artist William E. Sparks that sat atop the elevators in the ground-floor elevator lobby. The murals depicted colorful scenes from Pennsylvania history. The elevator doors themselves were pieces of art, decorated with heavy metal rosettes.

> *I will never forget the elevators and the incredible artwork above them, which shared the history. Pennsylvania history, Quaker history. You felt like you were arriving somewhere important every day.*
> —*Gina Major, events and public relations 1980–84*[138]

Giant marble columns separated different merchandise displays on the ground floor, and brass chandeliers hung from the ceiling, providing an abundance of light.

S&C Associate Susan Kearney remembers her first time going to the Eighth and Market store as a child with her mother in the late 1960s. "I remember being overwhelmed.…Oh, this is the Ritz, it doesn't get any better than this!"[139]

> *I was so fortunate I was there during the heyday of retailing. The store was so beautiful. When I first started working at the Store in 1972, I went to the fine jewelry department. The dark wood jewelry cases were beautiful as were the brass chandeliers above. I bought my first fine piece of jewelry with my paycheck, a gold bangle bracelet for $72.*
> —*Barbara McNutt, stationery buyer, 1978–83*[140]

No one in heels will ever forget the old wooden escalator that led down to the store's basement bargain area. Although it could have been replaced with a more modern elevator, the company held on to it as a link to its past (a novelty or hazard, depending on who you asked!).

The tenth floor was home to administrative and executive offices and could be accessed by an express elevator from the ground floor of the store. Here, one encountered people walking hurriedly across the black-and-white porcelain-tiled floor and past a large photo mural of the Philadelphia skyline that decorated the elevator lobby wall. The tenth floor was also home to the corporate offices, or "Mahogany Row," as many employees referred to it. "We called them the 'big shots,'" said Roy Miller, who worked down the hall in advertising.[141] In the 1980s and 1990s, Stockton, Peter and Francis Strawbridge occupied Mahogany Row, each with their own assistant stationed outside of their spacious offices, which were well lit by large windows looking down onto Market Street. It wasn't uncommon for employees to see the mayor, local elected officials or visiting celebrities pass through the tenth-floor lobby on their way into or out of a meeting with Stockton.

Sandra Jackson, copy chief in the Advertising Department, remembers lots of people coming to see Stockton. "He was a well-known businessman." One day, while waiting to take the elevator downstairs from the tenth floor, she was greeted by Stockton Strawbridge and Bob Hope getting off the elevator. "Bob Hope was a lot shorter than I thought he would be," said Sandra.[142]

Also on the tenth floor was the History Gallery, where customers and employees could read about the origins of the company and its founders. On display were old photographs and memorabilia, including a glass-encased antique cash register, one of the first used by Sales Associates.

Store Hours

The company grappled with store hours and holidays throughout its history. Frank Veale writes in *Family Business: The Momentous Seventies*, "Hours are a sensitive issue with us."[143] Stockton was quoted as saying, "I hate extended hours."[144] Preserving personal and family time was a value that the company held tight to for as long as it could. On Christmas Eve, frantic last-minute shoppers were ushered out of the store at five o'clock in the afternoon.

> *No ifs, ands or buts. S&C recognized employees had lives, too….The service managers came around to close. That's the only time I ever saw the managers not totally accommodate the customer.*
> *—Ray Pascali, sales associate 1979–84*[145]

Unlike many retailers, the store remained closed on December 26 until the 1970s. S&C was also one of the last department stores to stay closed on Memorial Day, until 1976.

Initially, Wednesday nights were the only night of the week that had evening shopping hours. By the 1960s, additional weekdays were added at both the Eighth and Market store and branch stores.

As the 1970s wore on, S&C succumbed to external pressure. The Gallery opened its doors on August 11, 1977. The large indoor shopping center was

In September 1946, the company reduced the work week from forty-four hours to forty hours, without making any adjustments to employee salaries.* This change likely came in response to the Fair Labor Standards Act, which passed Congress in 1938, establishing a forty-four-hour work week. The act was amended in 1949, reducing the work week to forty hours.

_____
* Lief, *Family Business*, 241.

meant to revitalize the Center City retail district along Market Street. Stockton Strawbridge had actively supported the development of the Gallery through his own fundraising efforts and political networking. Not only did it house several small retailers and restaurants, but it also had entrances to S&C, Gimbels and JCPenney. For S&C to stay competitive with its neighbors, it ultimately had to match their extended hours.

It was with more than a little reluctance, then, that on July 6, 1977, Stockton announced, "Despite long standing opposition to the extension of store hours, S&C will be open at its mid-town location Monday through Friday evenings from 10 to 9 (in addition to Wednesday nights), and on Sundays from noon to 5pm."[146]

All the Clover stores and some of the branch stores were already open for business on Sundays at this point, but Eighth and Market had always remained closed (perhaps out of respect to S&C's Quaker founders). August 14, 1977, would mark the first time the store was open on a Sunday.

Goodwill

Charitable giving was a long-held company value. Herbert Tily reflected on this in his speech he gave during a special dinner on December 18, 1929, celebrating his fifty years with S&C: "The merchant who is not civic minded is blindly self-centered. A merchant can prosper only in proportion as his community prospers."[147]

S&C employees put this value into practice time and again, which served to strength their Store Family bonds.

The Goodwill Association was created in the early twentieth century to raise funds to cover basic needs for the store's girl and boy messengers. Costs for dentist, doctor and optician visits along with clothes and milk and eggs were reported as disbursements for the fund in July 1911. Boys were also treated to a vacation at the YMCA summer camp in New Jersey.[148]

S&C Associates contributed thousands of dollars each year to the United Way, with which the company had a longstanding relationship dating to 1931.[149] The company-wide fundraising campaign was held every fall to benefit hundreds of Delaware Valley nonprofit organizations.

For over thirty years, S&C took part in the Christmas Shopping Tour, an event held for underserved children. Children between the ages of five and eight were given money to purchase holiday gifts for their loved ones. Accompanied by S&C and Clover volunteer chaperones, children got to roam the aisles of the Eighth and Market store. After shopping, they were treated to refreshments in the employee cafeteria and a visit with Santa.[150]

In the 1990s, Clover stores hosted a Senior and Disabled Citizens' Holiday Shopping Night. Stores opened at seven o'clock in the evening to thousands of customers for one night of holiday shopping in December. Assistance was provided by volunteers, coupons were given out, door prizes were awarded, carols were sung, baked goods and refreshments were available and shoppers could have their picture taken with Santa.

S&C's Echelon branch store had a long-running tradition that started in the 1970s of hosting an annual breakfast for children with disabilities from surrounding South Jersey schools, which took place in early December. Children received a candy-filled stocking to take home after enjoying breakfast, games, songs and a visit with Santa. The idea came from Francis R. Strawbridge, who was the store manager at the time. He suggested Associates spend their time and money on a local charity in lieu of sending Christmas cards to one another.[151]

In addition to these store- and company-wide campaigns, there are countless examples of how employees expressed goodwill to one another. In 1993, employees of S&C's Carpenter Shop volunteered their time outside of work hours to build a garage for the family of their fellow S&C carpenter Tommy Wilson. Tommy had started building the garage for his wife and three children but, sadly, died of cancer in November 1992. The group of S&C carpenters spent two days finishing the job in Tommy's memory.[152]

S&C CLUBS

In addition to sports teams, social clubs were a popular pastime of S&C employees. Formed and managed by employees, clubs expressed a wide array of interests, some of which clearly date themselves. There was the

Proscenium Club, which started in 1906 for employees who wished to perfect their speech and dramatic talents. The S&C Orchestra, which held dances for employees and their families, formed around the same time. There must have been several organ enthusiasts to start the Organ Club in 1958. The First Night Club treated members to discounted tickets to live performances at the Walnut Street and Forrest Theaters. The Business Belles, which was formed in the 1950s by the company rather than the employees, sought to "bring to the working woman the know-how that will enable her to organize every phase of her busy life."[153] Instead of providing tips and tools for better time management, which many women probably would have been eager to receive, the club focused on topics like how to entertain guests and set a table.

Perhaps the most recognized club inside and outside the Store Family was the chorus. Formed in October 1904 by employees who wanted to entertain their "fellows," it successfully did so throughout the life of S&C. Herbert Tily, a self-taught musician, was the first conductor. The club was open to both trained and untrained musicians of all ages and from all parts of the company. The first performance was held at the Philadelphia Academy of Music in March 1905 for the twenty-fifth anniversary of the employee Relief Association. The chorus boasted more than one hundred members in its first year. It went on to hold two annual performances: a spring concert at the Academy of Music for S&C employees, which doubled as an annual fundraiser for the Pension Fund Association, and a summer concert at Willow Grove Park, which was free and open to the public. On April 26, 1906, an exception was made for a third concert as a special benefit for survivors of the San Francisco earthquake. Customers and employees alike enjoyed the annual in-store Christmas performance during the holiday shopping season. The chorus gained considerable praise in its early years. It attracted guest performances by well-known singers and conductors and positive reviews in the local newspapers. In the 1960s, summer concerts were held at the Fairmont Park amphitheater as part of the Philadelphia Orchestra's outdoor concert series.

By the 1980s, the chorus was operating as the company's goodwill ambassador, performing at nursing homes, orphanages, military hospitals and homes for those with disabilities and terminal illnesses. Other performances were held at shopping malls where S&C stores were located and during the company's employee Christmas Eve celebration and the chorus's end-of-season concert at the Valley Forge Memorial Chapel.

STRAWBRIDGE & CLOTHIER CHORUS AT WILLOW GROVE, JUNE 16th, 1913.

Above: S&C Chorus at Willow Grove, 1913. *Courtesy of the author.*

Left: S&C Chorus, 1987. *Courtesy of the author.*

EMPLOYEE RECOGNITION

The company understood how important it was to formally recognize not just those Associates who stood out in their performance but also those who had demonstrated a long-term commitment to the Store Family. There were several special events throughout the year to honor these family members. Courtesy luncheons, which began in 1908, were held for any employee recognized for exceptional customer service. At the fiftieth anniversary of the courtesy luncheons in 1958, Frank Veale, newly promoted to vice president of operations and personnel, said, "An invitation to a Courtesy Luncheon is given for outstanding courtesy whether it is displayed on the First Floor, the Third Floor, in the Credit Department or on the Elevators."[154] The housekeeping staff and nightly cleaning crew were honored with an annual breakfast.[155] Annual luncheons also took place for members of the sponsor system, which paired new employees with more experienced ones. There were also award receptions. The STAR (Storewide Top Associate Recognition) Awards started in 1985. All branch stores participated in recognizing sales and sales-supporting staff who earned top productivity figures and good customer service records. There was an award given by the company's food services manager for Most Profitable Restaurant. Awards were given for top merchandising achievements, as well as for Buyer of the Year, Divisional of the Year, Department Manager of the Year and Major Executive of the Year. Clover employees were recognized for their outstanding performance each year during the Best of the Best awards.

Awards were also given to employees for their help with identifying theft and security problems. Clyde Williams from housekeeping received twenty-five dollars in 1958 for turning in a customer for shoplifting in the Men's Clothing Department.[156]

Employees of the Personnel Department fondly remember the David Awards, which were held each year during the 1980s and 1990s by vice president for personnel David Strawbridge. Former S&C Associates Karen Kane and Nancy O'Donnell described it as a fun take on the Oscars. Awards were given to Associates and managers in specific categories, like Best Supporting Systems Trainer.

In 1988, the company started to recognize employee achievements in clubs and athletics with the Activities Banquet. By then, over seven hundred employees were spending their non-working hours participating in company-sponsored activities.[157]

50th Courtesy Luncheon Held July 3rd

This page, top: Courtesy luncheon, 1958. *Courtesy of the author.*

This page, bottom: STAR Awards recipients, 1994. *Courtesy of the author.*

Opposite, top: Barbara Rittenhouse accepts Buyer of the Year award from Peter Strawbridge, 1987. *Courtesy of the author.*

Opposite, bottom: Human resources employees Karen Kane and Nancy O'Donnell Abbot with VP for personnel David Strawbridge at one of the annual David Awards. *Courtesy of Nancy O'Donnell Abbot.*

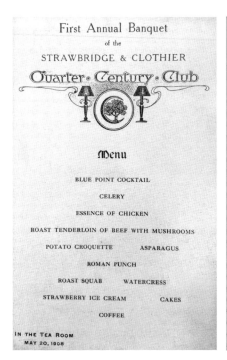

First Annual Banquet
of the
STRAWBRIDGE & CLOTHIER
Quarter · Century · Club

Menu

BLUE POINT COCKTAIL

CELERY

ESSENCE OF CHICKEN

ROAST TENDERLOIN OF BEEF WITH MUSHROOMS

POTATO CROQUETTE   ASPARAGUS

ROMAN PUNCH

ROAST SQUAB   WATERCRESS

STRAWBERRY ICE CREAM   CAKES

COFFEE

IN THE TEA ROOM
MAY 20, 1908

Join the

Quarter Century Club

Members of this unique organization have so many courtesies shown them that every Employe should make up his or her mind to become one of them.

No Dues

A Banquet

A Week's Vacation in Winter

So far it has a membership of only 154, but new members are joining every year.

Every employe in the house, except minors, is eligible for membership.

Every one should join this unique organization —when you can.

Any member will tell you how you can join.

Left: Menu for the first Quarter Century Club banquet, 1908. *Courtesy of the Hagley Museum and Library.*

Right: Quarter Century Club ad, 1913 *Store Chat*. *Courtesy of the author.*

Joining hands singing "Auld Lang Syne" are from left, Margaret Deak, Francis R. Strawbridge, David W. Strawbridge, Margaret Clews, Peter S. Strawbridge, Blake Bass and Warren White.

Quarter Century Club banquet, 1985. *Courtesy of the author.*

New Quarter Century Club members enjoying the evening, 1985. *Courtesy of the author.*

The list of awards and recognition ceremonies could go on; however, the most anticipated event of the year was the Quarter Century Club banquet. Founded in 1908 at the suggestion of general manager Herbert Tily, it was a way to promote "good fellowship" among employees who had been with the company for twenty-five years or more.[158] At its beginning, it had 85 members, 36 of whom were women. There were no dues to belong, and a governing committee was formed, which organized the annual banquet. In 1915, there were over 150 members in the club. By the time the company was sold in 1996, it boasted approximately 300 members and approximately 6 who had been with the company for fifty years or more.

The Quarter Century Club banquets were typically held in September in the Corinthian Dining Room with live music, a full-course sit-down dinner, an emcee (often a company officer and member of one of the founding families) and a guest of honor. It was not unusual for festivities to run well into the night. Toasts and roasts filled the room with laughter. Tears were even shed as the careers and contributions of any S&C or Clover employee spanning twenty-five years were lauded and praised. Along with the celebration, members received a commemorative pin and extra vacation days.

I recall when Bob Hoffner, Clover's VP for Stores became eligible for membership we played a prank on him. He was quite gullible. There was always a band, music, and dancing at the Banquet. We made up a dance

*card for Bob with the names of several S&C female members on it. He
dutifully went to the first name on the card and found out about the trick—
to our enjoyment.*
—*Warren White, executive VP and general manager, Clover division*[159]

For those who reached fifty years in the family, a gold watch was gifted to
them during a special luncheon, also held in the Corinthian Dining Room.

A QUARTER CENTURY AND COUNTING

In 1908, Wilfred Keely was chosen as the
first president of the Quarter Century
Club. At the time, he was a forty-year
veteran of S&C and the longest-serving
employee. Wilfred started his career
in 1865 before Justus partnered with
Isaac. He was a Civil War regimental
quartermaster sergeant, and Justus hired
him fresh from the battlefield to be his
cashier and bookkeeper. He also gave
him a place to sleep in a back room on
the second floor for three months.[160]

Wilfred H. Keely. *Courtesy of
the Hagley Museum and Library.*

Mary Byrne was the longest actively
employed Store Family member to work
in the same department in the history of the company. She started
her S&C career at the Eighth and Market store on November 4,
1929, and was assigned to the Stationery Department, where she
remained for sixty-five years until retiring in 1994. At the time of
her retirement, she was one of the few living employees who had
worked in the store before the 1932 remodel. When interviewed
for an issue of *Store Chat* in 1990 to honor her sixtieth anniversary
with the company, she recalled how the old building was smaller.
"It reminded me of a big barn with big cases on the walls and dark,
hardwood floors. Merchandise was folded on tables." Mary also
recalled the strict dress code of the time and that saleswomen had

Special luncheon in honor of Mary Byrne's sixty years at S&C. *From left*: Steven and Peter Strawbridge, Mary Byrne, Francis and David Strawbridge, 1990. *Courtesy of the author.*

to wear dark blue or black dresses in the winter. She was extremely nervous when she came to work one day wearing a blue dress with white polka dots. "My manager sent me to Personnel because the polka dots couldn't be larger than a dime."[161] Fortunately, her polka dots were the right size.

For her retirement, the company treated Mary and a friend to a Bermuda cruise organized by S&C's Recreational Association. She almost didn't make it back home. Too busy shopping during a stop in the town of Hamilton, she and her friend missed the eleven o'clock boarding time. They had failed to set their watches an hour ahead to Bermuda time and didn't realize it until they saw their ship backing away from the dock. After some time panicking, they received help from a local tugboat captain who volunteered to take the two women out to sea to meet their ship. To the shock and amazement of fellow S&C Associates on board the cruise, Mary and her friend were seen climbing a long rope from the tugboat up the side of the ship. An S&C associate was quoted in *Store Chat* as mumbling to a friend, "I just saw Mary Byrne on a tugboat, out there." A harrowing incident but a hilarious one, too. Mary said she couldn't stop laughing; her friend, however, cried.[162]

Advertising was another way in which the company recognized its employees. People who grew up in the Delaware Valley in the 1980s might recall the peppy S&C jingle "Strawbridge & Clothier, Oh, What a Difference!" First debuted in 1983, the new S&C advertising slogan highlighted its employee talent and trustworthy customer service—once again, setting S&C employees apart from its competitors. "Our Associates do make a difference" was proudly displayed in S&C advertisements that featured employees in a range of positions, from sales associate to housekeeping staff to Food Hall server to ombudsman.[163]

"Oh, What a Difference!" ads, 1980s. *Courtesy of the author.*

STORE CHAT

Perhaps the most effective way the company recognized the professional and personal achievements of its large family was through the employee magazine, *Store Chat*. First published in June 1906, it was another idea birthed from the fruitful mind of Herbert Tily. Then general manager of the company, Tily hoped it could be "a means of binding the 5,000 employees in close harmony."[164] This sentiment was echoed in the preamble of early issues:

> *Edited by and in the interest of the employes* [sic] *of Strawbridge & Clothier and published for them occasionally, in the hope of promoting the general welfare and bringing each into closer relations with all.*

Uncertain of *Store Chat*'s longevity, the inaugural issue cautioned that "Store Chat is a fledgling—an experiment. Its success, even its continued existence, will depend upon the interest with which it is received by our fellow employes [*sic*]."

Tily and the newsletter's first editors should feel proud that the experiment was fully embraced by S&C employees. The publication continued to be produced each month and eventually biquarterly until the sale of the company. The only disruption came during the Great Depression, when publication ceased between 1932 and 1943 as a cost-saving measure. The magazine gained broad notoriety outside of S&C and was used as a model by other retailers and businesses. "Henry Selfridge, of Selfridges, the first American department store to open in London…sent for copies of *Store Chat* to pattern a store publication for his 4,000 employees."[165]

Throughout *Store Chat*'s existence, readers could peruse a variety of employee-related news, including announcements about births, deaths, illnesses, retirements, engagements, weddings, new clubs and sports teams and S&C Chorus concerts; tributes to long-serving employees; fun facts about employee hobbies and charitable causes; and employee accounts of vacations at Wildwood, New Jersey, during the early twentieth century and, later, cruises and tours to places like Greece, Italy and Alaska that were organized by S&C's own employee travel agent. Photographs and cartoons were mixed in with articles.

Readers could also learn about various transformations and advancements of their growing company, like store expansions; the 1932 remodel of the Eighth and Market store; branch store openings; the new Clover division;

buying trips to new countries; new uniforms and practices of Corinthian Room restaurant staff; the introduction of the store's telephone system, installed in 1905 to serve the increasing number of customers who were shopping by phone; and the installation of the addressing machine, rolled out in 1906, which could address three thousand catalogues in an hour, cash registers, elevators and the RCA 301 computer, which was installed at Eighth and Market in 1963, making S&C the first retail store in the city to have one.

Employees read about benefits programs. Reports frequently appeared from the savings fund, the Relief Association and the pension fund. Later *Store Chat* issues featured quarterly reports about company contributions to health care packages and retirement plans. Company-wide charitable drives for United Way and other organizations were promoted, as was the purchase of war bonds during World War I and World War II.

> *It was the glue, it was our in-house newspaper. From cover to cover you saw people from other stores, celebrate quarter century members, or special messages from the Strawbridges. It was a way to know the players. Even if we didn't work with them side by side, we knew everyone everywhere. It was a way to keep people together and make them feel good about their accomplishments.*
> —Dorette Rota Jackson, Store Chat *editor 1987–96*[166]

Improving employee conduct and productivity were common themes, especially in issues from the first two decades. Scholar Jerome P. Bjelopera describes how readers of *Store Chat* and other department store newsletters were "bombarded with articles, poems, and first-hand accounts declaring that model clerical employees loved hard work, embodied thriftiness and loyalty to the firm, and led temperate lives."[167]

Poems and inspirational quotes were peppered throughout early issues, along with messages and short essays promoting good health, fitness and hygiene. Readers could find titles like "Habits and Their Results" and "Best Sleep Before Midnight."

"Suggestions on Salesmanship" was an article in the October 1906 issue and included:

> *When a customer inquires for an article it is seldom wise to ask what price she wishes to pay. Many people appreciate the compliment of being shown more expensive goods than they usually purchase: no one likes to be considered "cheap."*

STRAWBRIDGE & CLOTHIER STORE CHAT

| VOLUME I. | Philadelphia, June, 1906. | NUMBER 1 |

EDITED BY AND IN THE INTEREST OF THE EMPLOYES OF STRAWBRIDGE & CLOTHIER AND PUBLISHED FOR THEM OCCASIONALLY, IN THE HOPE OF PROMOTING THE GENERAL WELFARE AND BRINGING EACH INTO CLOSER RELATIONS WITH ALL.

THE FIRST WORD.

STORE CHAT is a fledgling—an experiment. Its success, even its continued existence, will depend upon the interest with which it is received by our fellow-employes.

Its purpose is to afford a means of interchange of news and views both entertaining and instructive. It is just as much yours as anybody's, and each employe who has any thing interesting to say is invited to say it in STORE CHAT.

This store's "population" is equal to that of many a proud little city. None of us know all the rest of us. While no other large store organization is more closely related as to its units, we should know each other better, and some of us should know the store better.

We hope to issue STORE CHAT periodically, expecting improvement and growing interest with each succeeding number. It can be made helpful to every one of us if every one of us helps.

It is expected that this will prove a most effective medium for presenting important matters relative to the store service—a means of communication from management to employes, as well as between employes.

In these pages will be found, from time to time, records of individual employes whose work has been of such a standard of excellence as to entitle them to particular mention as distinguished members of this mercantile household.

Boxes have been placed in the coat rooms as receptacles for suggestions and criticisms touching any part of our store life, and for any items which you may desire to contribute to STORE CHAT. Use them freely!

OUR CHORUS AT WILLOW GROVE.

Congratulations to the Chorus!

And that ovation's unanimous. Like the well-conducted household that we are, the whole store-family's glad of the success of any part of it. The laurels our talented members captured at Willow Grove appeal to our sense of family pride—a chaplet of conquest on the entire store's brow.

It was a night, it was a scene, it was a production to be remembered—always. The harmony of 150 voices blending with the Damrosch Orchestra, the setting of sky, trees and flowers painted by Nature's incomparable hand. And the whole scene obedient to the Director's baton as at the command of some magic wand. *Encore!*

OUR WINDOW BOXES.

A success from the moment they surprised delighted eyes that May morning when they bloomed "all of a sudden" on the store front.

Everybody thinks them beautiful. And, *"What a happy thought!"* many have said. That touch of living green on the stately, dignified store-facade is like a smile irradiating a face. The trailing vines swaying in the breeze seem hands beckoning welcome to the store. Often must the eyes of passing pedestrians pause with pleasure in the contemplation of the line of growing green—a cheery greeting in the handwriting of Nature—that surprises in the very heart of the built-up city.

And to town-tired eyes, to the toil-worn brain, perhaps to burdened hearts, the geraniums laughing in the sun and the vines dancing in the breeze may conjure visions of glad, green country, waken hopes of boy-

Cover page of the first *Store Chat. Courtesy of the Hagley Museum and Library.*

In addressing a woman the word "Madame" should be used in preference to "Lady." To a man the salutation, "Sir," is correct.

Tips for female Sales Associates on good grooming and not letting your slip show were given in issues from the 1950s and 1960s.

Cartoons and stories about comical interactions with customers were also featured. The following accounts come from the June 1906 issue:

Among other questions asked by one employing a boy, the other day, was this: "What does your father do?" To which he readily replied, "He drinks."

Gentleman, intending to buy a silk waist, accosts saleslady with query, "Are you engaged?" She hesitated for a moment, as she thought it a very delicate question; however, she managed to say "No," and was surprised to hear a lady at her side say that she was "perfectly willing to be."

A customer asked to see a particular pair of shoes in a size 10. The Sales Associate regrettably informed her that the largest size he had was a 7½. "That's fine," the customer responded. "I'll try on those."

Entertaining accounts were shared by employees in later *Store Chat* issues like these from May–June 1989:

A customer became quite upset when she thought an Associate was being less than accommodating in accepting her bill payment. "What do you mean I can't pay my Sears bill here?" she snapped.

An elderly customer brought his own bread into the Store to make sure the toaster he wanted to purchase worked to his liking. He then proceeded to eat the toast as the Associate rang up the sale!

Comical stories aside, *Store Chat* also served as a historical record. It captured not just the company's growth and transformation over the decades but the country's as well. Economic, political, social and technological events and changes were all woven into the stories and articles. It's a twentieth-century history of the United States through the lens of a retailer.

FAMILY FUN

In 1937, Frederic Strawbridge moved from Torworth to a new house in Chestnut Hill. Developers purchased the estate to make way for Alden Park Manor, a three-towered, 270-apartment complex that catered to the rich. The original mansion remained on the property and was converted into the Alden Park Inn. Sadly, the building burned in a fire in 1979.* Isaac Clothier's estate, Ballytore, still stands today in its original Wynnewood location. It now functions as the Saint Sahag and Saint Mesrob Armenian Church.

Throughout the life of the company, employees were invited several times a year to unwind and socialize at annual picnics and outings. Isaac Clothier hosted an annual Fourth of July outing for all employees at his estate, Ballytore, located in the suburban town of Wynnewood. It was from the fun and games at these outings that the idea for a company athletic field grew.[168] Justus Strawbridge hosted a garden party for saleswomen at Torworth, his twenty-acre estate located in Philadelphia's Germantown neighborhood. In the summer of 1907, Justus's son Frederic Strawbridge, who resided at Torworth, opened the grounds to all S&C employees on Saturday afternoons during July and August. Employees were welcome to walk through the grounds, play tennis or croquet, swing or enjoy the hammocks. Refreshments were also served. A *Store Chat* announcement for the event noted, "The only restrictions: Do not climb trees or pull flowers."[169]

Picnics and gatherings continued long after Torworth and Ballytore were no more. The annual golf outing was held for all company employees. The annual executive outing for Clover and S&C executives included volleyball games and a barbecue, and at the Clover management picnic, employees enjoyed softball, relay races and other games. Many of the employee clubs and sports leagues, such as the chorus and softball league, had their own annual social gatherings.

* Oscar Beisert (architectural historian), "Nomination of Historic Building, Structure, Site or Object: Philadelphia Register of Historic Places," http://keepingphiladelphia.org/wp-content/uploads/2019/06/5710-Wissahickon-ave-FINAL-w-FORM.pdf.

Fourth of July annual outing, 1883. *Courtesy of the Hagley Museum and Library.*

Annual golf outing, 1986. *Courtesy of the author.*

The Anniversary Sale Rally

Outside of Clover Day, the Anniversary Sale was the store's most anticipated sales event of the year. Held each June since the beginning of the company, the sale was celebrated with parades and other festivities to attract shoppers and motivate employees. In 1949, Stockton Strawbridge bumped the start of the sale to May. Intending to make the sale more successful, he collaborated with Ella Waters, S&C's public relations director, on incorporating friendly competition and theatrical antics. Branch stores, divisions, buyers and department managers all competed for best sales. The winners received an award for their hard work from a company officer at the Anniversary Awards Luncheon. The pinnacle of the weekslong event was the much-anticipated Anniversary Sale Rally. Egos were likely checked as company executives became the source of hilarious entertainment that often brought the house down. The show revolved around a musical theme that changed year to year, such as "S&C Goes to the Movies," "Anniversary Tales" (a fairy tales and storybook theme) and "Back to the Future." Although each branch held its own rally in its store auditorium, it was the rally held in the large auditorium at Eighth and Market Street that was the hot ticket. Associates from all parts of the company piled into the auditorium, easily filling its eight-hundred-person capacity for all three shows, which featured the officers of the company and Justus's great-grandsons, Francis, Peter, David and Steven. The showstopper in 1984 was their performance of Michael Jackson's "Beat It," when they moonwalked across the stage in black-and-red leather jackets.

The last rally was held in 1990. Sadly, changing market conditions forced the company to implement tough cost-cutting decisions to stay afloat, which meant saying farewell to the annual rally.

The main purpose of the Anniversary Rally was to stir up excitement in the employees for this once-a-year sale. I have a feeling that a secondary, but not stated purpose, was to make the "bosses" of the Store act like perfect fools in front of the whole Store!
—*Steven L. Strawbridge, VP treasurer and secretary*[170]

Every June, I think about anniversary weekend and the plays. Nobody cared what they did in front of other people; it was something that brought us all together.
—*Debbie Herron Jeffreys, merchandise information trainer, 1983–87*[171]

Store Chat cover for the 1988 Anniversary Sale Rally. *Courtesy of the author.*

Above: Anniversary Sale Rally performances, 1958. *Courtesy of the author.*

Left: The fourth generation performs at the Anniversary Sale Rally. *Clockwise from top left*: Steven, David, Francis, Peter. 1987. *Courtesy of the author.*

Ella Waters at an S&C Anniversary Sale Rally. *Courtesy of the Hagley Museum and Library.*

For eighteen years, the Anniversary Sale Rally was produced and directed by Ella Waters. She started her decades-long career at S&C in 1934 as fashion director and ended it in 1967 as director of public relations and special events. Among her many S&C achievements was launching Philadelphia's first fashion show held inside a department store in 1936.[172] Ella was known for her big smile and "infectious enthusiasm" and summed up her passion for retail with the quote, "There is no business-like store business where you stay young because you have fun."[173]

S&C SALES EVENTS

In addition to the Anniversary Sale, S&C held other promotional sales throughout the year. There were Big Saturdays, which occurred once a month, and the Warehouse Sale, which happened several times a year, allowing shoppers to take advantage of steep sale prices at S&C's large distribution center in south Philadelphia.

> *The sale prices were drop dead, can't get anything better than that. I think I bought everything for my house.*
> —*Clem Pascarella, S&C stock office, 1977–89*[174]

> *I remember my first warehouse sale. When the doors opened, the people who were lined up outside, they ran into the store right for the item they wanted. At the beginning it scared me. But I got used it.*
> —*Ray Pascali, S&C Sales Associate, 1979–84*[175]

But no sale was as popular or as long running as Clover Day. Herbert Tily was the brainchild, conceiving the idea in 1906. The first Clover Day was held on March 29, 1906, and was deemed a "good-luck day" for customers. Rather than having a designated sale area in the store, merchandise that had been marked down to its lowest price of the year was scattered throughout the store, and customers would have to search for it as if searching for a lucky four-leaf clover.

S&C officer Frank Veale confidently declared in his book *Family Business: Strawbridge & Clothier: The Momentous Seventies* that Clover Day might have been the longest continuously held and most successful regular monthly sale day in the history of the American department store.[176]

I had never heard of Clover Day when I started at S&C. I was 19 and told I had to work Clover Day. I was put in the basement. I'd never seen so many people in all my life. The ladies changed to football players, knocking over each other. Outside the streets were packed, you couldn't

Warehouse sale. *Courtesy of the Hagley Museum and Library.*

Left: Clover Day advertisement. *Courtesy of the Hagley Museum and Library.*

Below: Clover Day shoppers. *Courtesy of the Hagley Museum and Library.*

walk on the sidewalk. That was my last Clover Day. I said no the following year when asked. These are little nice ladies that go to church every Sunday. You live and learn.
—Roy Miller, S&C graphic designer & illustrator, Advertising Department, 1968–96[177]

S&C and Unions

Our intent is to keep all lines of communication open so that it will never be necessary for you to feel that a third party, such as a labor union, is necessary in this Company.
—S&C employee handbook 1987

Philadelphia has been a labor town ever since the country's first labor union, the Shoemaker's Union, formed in 1794. Despite operating in a city with such proud labor roots, S&C strove to provide its employees with benefits packages and working conditions that would leave them with little need for a union. This was not an unusual approach for department stores, especially in the early twentieth century. Retail historian Vicki Howard writes that by the 1920s, "benefits that could placate workers, reduce the notoriously high turnover rates in the industry, and help avoid unionization likely seemed a reasonable operating expense."[178] Employee benefits also helped to improve the reputations of retailers as good employers.

Although Sales Associates at S&C stores and Clover stores did not belong to a union, outside efforts to get employees to organize were not uncommon. In March 1971, the Retail Clerks International union unsuccessfully tried to encourage Sales Associates at the company's new Clover division to join its ranks. Frank Veale recalled, "They want desperately to move in early while Clover is only beginning to grow, and before our new Clover associates have fully learned what kind of company we are—or try to be."[179]

The few employees that were union included kitchen and waitstaff at the Corinthian Room and the employee cafeteria staff at the Eighth and Market store. Restaurant staff at S&C branch stores and Clover stores were not unionized. In a highly unusual move, in 1983, two waitresses from the Corinthian Room asked to decertify from their union. Joe Nimerfroh, who was director of labor relations and benefits for the company at the time, said, "The waitresses and kitchen workers were getting all S&C benefits and appropriate wages and really were getting nothing extra for their $35 per month union dues."[180] He remembers that after several months of employee meetings and reviewing National Labor Relations Board guidelines, a vote was taken, and a majority of the restaurant, kitchen and cafeteria staff agreed to decertify their union membership.

Other union jobs were held by S&C's truck drivers, warehouse workers and employees of men's alterations at the Eighth and Market store. In 1938, S&C lost its contract with the truck drivers' union when it, along with several other local department stores, failed to meet the union's demands. From the beginning, S&C offered free home delivery to customers. The company had its own distinctive fleet of horse-drawn green delivery trucks with vermilion trim, which were later replaced by motorized trucks. The loss of the union contract meant the store had to retire its handsome trucks and instead contract with UPS's brown trucks and, later, a local trucking company. By 1972, S&C switched to the U.S. Postal Service for its deliveries. As for the "free" part, customers sadly said goodbye to that perk in 1979 due to growing costs.[181]

Although the company no longer had to negotiate with truck drivers after 1938, its warehouse employees remained unionized. The company's warehouse, which was referred to as the Distribution Center, had long been located on Poplar Street. With the growth of branch stores and greater demand for merchandise, it was clear by the mid-1960s that a much larger and more modernized Distribution Center was needed. In 1969, S&C broke ground on a 26.5-acre site in South Philadelphia. The employees of the Distribution Center were members of the Brotherhood of Teamsters Local No. 169, which had an aggressive reputation, at least among the S&C officers who had to deal with it. To say that the company dreaded its contract negotiations with the Teamsters every three years would be an understatement. It was a stressful balancing act accompanied by sleepless nights and high blood pressure for all involved. In 1970, the first year of operation for the new Distribution Center, a strike was narrowly avoided. This would not be the case in June 1973, when the company became entangled in its first strike in thirty-five years—and an ugly one, at that.

For five long weeks, from early June to early July, picketers gathered outside of the Distribution Center, the Eighth and Market store and nearly all the branch locations.[182] Employees, customers and passersby were greeted with signs and loud, disparaging remarks about S&C and Stockton Strawbridge through bullhorns. Fortunately, an agreement was reached, but the damage had been done. The company's extended family had become fractured for all to see thanks to local and national news media coverage.

Frank Veale summed up the bitter experience when describing the 1973 strike:

> *There is very little pleasant about a strike—especially for a company like ours which prides itself on being a pleasant and comfortable place to work. You feel strange and awkward suddenly finding your path lined with picketing men whom ordinarily you are accustomed to greet with friendly recognition. It is almost embarrassing—and at times you wonder whether an old friend, now your adversary, might not be feeling a twinge of the same as he avoids your eye.*[183]

According to Joe Nimerfroh, by the 1980s, just under two hundred employees out of fifteen thousand were union.

CHAPTER 7

A WELL-OILED MACHINE

*But the store is an empty place without people. It takes people to move
merchandise, to sell, to buy it.... The jobs of our people are interdependent, each
woven into the other....It has been people, their talents, their ideas, their efforts
that moved this store forward.*
—Store Chat, *January 1958, ninetieth anniversary of S&C*

Following is a selection of quotes and memories from the many
different employees who kept the family functioning.

CLEM PASCARELLA

Stock Office

From 1977 to 1989, Clem Pascarella wore many different hats at S&C.
He started off on the twelfth floor of the Eighth and Market store in stock
and shipping and receiving. Eventually, he ended up working in stock on
every floor of the building. He knew all about the freight elevators and the
tunnel that connected the main store to the warehouse behind it on Filbert
Street. Everything that went to the branch stores was first filtered through
Eighth and Market. "It was a well-oiled working environment." The biggest
challenge was figuring out how to deliver merchandise to all ten branch
stores in one day. He would be gone until nine or ten o'clock in the evening
some days. Clem assisted the stock manager, collecting timecards and issuing

paychecks. He worked overtime on the selling floor during the holidays. That was his favorite job. "Taking care of the customer and making sure that we got what we needed to them. It was hectic; it gave me that rush that I needed." He even did odd jobs, such as driving Stockton Strawbridge to catch a flight at JFK Airport in New York. He recalls shoveling snow one winter day from the heliport on top of Eighth and Market—then going to shovel more snow eight miles away at Stockton's mother's large estate so the company helicopter could safely land in her yard to pick her up and take her to the Corinthian Room for lunch. It was a big effort, only for the ninety-seven-year-old matriarch to decide to forgo the journey at the last minute. Despite this day, Clem says he always felt valued. He recalls constant contact with the ownership. "We weren't treated like just another number; we were treated like a family member. Which no one does these days."[184]

Susan Kearney

Part-Time Sales Associate

Susan made sure to put on a professional appearance when she applied for a Sales Associate position at the Eighth and Market store in 1975. She was looking to earn extra money while in college at Temple. She wore her Sunday best. "I looked like a bright, shiny penny," she remembers. It paid off, because she was hired on the spot and assigned to the coveted third floor, where Misses and Juniors were located. Eventually, she was assigned to the Philadelphia Shop, which carried high-end designer clothing. "It was so much fun!" she said. Susan worked alongside three women who had been at S&C since right after World War II. "They would talk about what Philadelphia used to be like: the nightclubs, the men. They were hysterical.…They had some of the most ribald jokes. I called them 'the Ladies.'"

Dealing with the clientele was also entertaining. It wasn't unusual for a wealthy man to bring his mistress in for a shopping spree. Over time, the Ladies became familiar with who was the mistress and who was the wife. Susan remembered when both the mistress and the wife of one local celebrity were trying on clothes in the fitting room at the same time. She and the other Sales Associates did their best to make sure the two women didn't interact. "You had to learn how to handle the politics," joked Susan.

Overall, Susan said working in sales was a great way to see all kinds of people, all different walks of life, "how people are so similar yet so different."[185]

SANDRA JACKSON

Copy Chief, Advertising Department

Sandra Jackson remembers how much wider the newspapers were back in the 1960s and '70s. "The papers were huge and heavy with department store advertising." Wanamaker's, Gimbels, Lits and S&C all advertised in them.

Sandra came to S&C in 1968 as a proofreader. At that time, there were three newspapers in the city, the *Philadelphia Inquirer*, the *Daily News* and the *Bulletin*. "We were in the newspaper every day with pages and pages of advertising. There was the morning paper, then different ads for the evening paper." Nothing was done electronically then. Everything was typed, artists drew things and photos were rarely used. Sandra's job was to look for typos and other errors in the copy. She remembers how there was a lot of physical work involved. The copy for an ad would be written and proofread; the artwork would be laid out by the Art Department. Once the copy and artwork were completed, it was someone's job to run the ad over to the newspaper to produce a proof and then run it back to the Art Department. From there, the proof was sent to the buyer associated with the ad so they could make any necessary corrections. The corrections were then manually input onto the proof and sent back to the newspaper, which would send out another proof. "Most things went to two proofs, but sometimes it went to three or four proofs. Merchandise might arrive to the store but wouldn't match the drawing in the ad, or it was damaged or it didn't come in at all. Anything could delay finalizing the ad. The workday could be very long." Sandra was good at her job, though—so good that by the time she left S&C in 1981, she was the copy chief.[186]

ROSE (SHAW) PONTZ

Visual Displays

Rose Pontz worked in visual displays at the Exton branch store for twenty-nine years. It could be hard work and stressful at times, but she loved it. Along with dressing mannequins, she was responsible for displays in the Home Department. Bridal displays, bedding, table settings, kitchenware and housewares were all her areas of expertise. More than once, the

Exton store won company awards for its visual displays. Rose recalled that although the company set the theme for displays and provided stores with props and materials, "if you were creative, Strawbridge's would let you do what you want."[187]

Reverend Joseph W. Bongard

Service Manager

Before becoming a priest, Father Bongard began his S&C career working in sales in the Men's Department on the first floor of the Eighth and Market store. He was in college and looking for evening and weekend shifts. When the gallery opened and the store extended its evening hours, he was asked to become a service manager. He was trained to know every department in the thirteen-story store and the location of all the merchandise. Attention to customer service was paramount, though. He remembers Stockton Strawbridge's words: "When your name goes on my building, you can say no to a customer!"

Just a young man, he was given a tremendous amount of responsibility. "Here I was in college, and we had the responsibility of opening the doors in the morning, checking everybody in, at [the] end of the day checking everybody out, [closing] the doors."

Bongard's shifts were full of activity, leading meetings with Sales Associates about promotions, advising them on how to improve their customer service, assigning breaks, checking the cash registers and making sure charges were correctly entered, training Associates when the store switched from manual cash registers to computerized registers and constantly tidying up clothes that had been rummaged through by customers.

From 1977 to 1985, Bongard worked on every floor of the building. He continued working evenings and weekends while in seminary school. The first floor was his favorite. "It was always crowded," he said. He even enjoyed the crowds on Clover Days. "When I said, 'Open those doors,' the lobby would be packed with people, especially with November Clover Day. They were fun to work."

Now, as a priest in Philadelphia for more than thirty years, Father Bongard has had the honor and pleasure of marrying several S&C people over the years.[188]

GINA MAJOR

Public Relations and Special Events Manager

Gina had just graduated from Drexel University when she got a job at S&C in 1980. She started as a coordinator for the Teen Boards in the suburban branch stores. "The idea was to look for young women in high school who would help promote S&C through events inside the store and in community events outside the store," said Gina. In 1982, she was promoted to public relations and special events manager and began working out of the Eighth and Market store. Her four short years at S&C were packed full of event planning, including fashion shows, cooking demonstrations, celebrity visits and community events. "I worked at an extremely busy public relations office. Their outreach was huge. There was always something going on. Lots of life, lots of spirit, lots of activity beyond just selling."

Despite her demanding full-time S&C job, Gina found time to compete in local pageants. She competed in the Miss Pennsylvania Scholarship Pageant in 1980, followed by the Miss New Jersey Scholarship Pageant in 1982 and finally, again, in the Miss Pennsylvania Scholarship Pageant in 1984, which she won. Unfortunately, her success in the pageant meant she had to leave S&C to go on the road full time and prepare for the 1984 Miss America Competition. Gina shared that she proudly talked about S&C in her Miss America interview with Pearl Bailey. Nearly forty years later, Gina said that her time at S&C was "absolutely some of the best of my life."[189]

SUSAN ELFAND WIENER

Security, Cottman Avenue Clover Store

Susan began working at the Cottman Avenue Clover branch store while she was pursuing a business degree in college. It was the mid-1980s, and Clover had recently begun using a UPC scanning system at its checkout stations. Susan wrote a college paper on the conversion and had the opportunity to interview Clover executives in their corporate offices at Eighth and Market. After graduating, Susan decided to go to law school and returned to Clover for part-time work. She wanted to try a different position and applied to be a part-time security guard. Outside of on-the-job training, she didn't receive much to aid her in her new position. "They gave us a walkie-talkie that was probably the size of six cell phones by today's standards and a big handbag to put it in. No gun, no baton," she recalled. Susan's main responsibilities were accompanying the cash office representatives while they collected money from the cash registers and tracking suspicious people on the store's camera system—an onerous process, since the company had a strict policy that an individual could not be approached unless the security guard was positive they had stolen merchandise. This required moving quickly from the shopping floor where a suspected criminal was spotted to the office to replay the incident on the security camera. Unfortunately, the back-and-forth created enough time for many suspected shoplifters to get away. Even with these challenges, Susan successfully caught a shoplifter her first night on the job.

Although Susan was one of several young employees at the time, there were also many older employees at the store. Despite the age differences, she remembers being treated with respect. "I didn't feel like I was talked down to. The older employees were helpful." Susan made a lot of friends in her four years at Clover. She joined the softball team and enjoyed meeting colleagues for drinks at the bar across the street after work and dressing up for Halloween. "It was a real family atmosphere," she said.[190]

Marc Fox

Merchandise Handling Manager and Assistant Traffic Manager

Marc Fox started working in the service building at S&C in 1987. He managed service operations for the twelfth and thirteenth floors at Eighth and Market, which were considered part of the service building, and later, the third, fifth and sixth floors. As manager of the floors, he led a team of floor supervisors, area leaders and Associates whose primary responsibilities were to check the goods against the purchase order (PO) to make sure the quantity, color, size and all other details were correct. Marc's team also applied the price tags and distributed the goods to the branch stores per the buyer's plan. Marc recalls that the service building was very hot in the summer; only the manager's office had air conditioning. In the heat of the summer, extra work breaks, called "heat breaks," were given to the Associates.

Later in his career, Marc became the assistant traffic manager and worked with the truckers, provided shipping instructions to vendors and led the team that paid freight bills and filed claims for damaged goods. "I also started a Vendor Compliance Program during this time. There, I would manage a program where vendors were charged a penalty for incorrect shipping (late, wrong size, color, etc. versus PO). This program recovered hundreds of thousands of dollars for the company when a vendor was noncompliant with the PO instructions.

"The group of people I worked with in the Service Building were some of the best people I have worked with throughout my career. We had a lot of laughs and worked well together. My fellow managers, Peter Bertolino, Ken Low, Sheila Frison and the late Fred Martucci, Andy Couch and Ed Schmitt, should also be recognized. I would be remiss if I did not mention long-time floor supervisors Carl Reid, Lou Titano, Jose Abreu, Jean Davis and Ann Ford and those I can't recall who were part of the backbone of the Service Building during this time."[191]

RON AVELLINO

VP for Planning, Property Management and Development

Ron began his thirty-seven-year career with S&C as one of seven assistant buyers in the Toy Department. He worked every single day from Thanksgiving to Christmas, including Saturdays and Sundays. After serving in a variety of assistant buyer and buyer positions, he became the store manager for the Springfield branch, replacing Francis R. Strawbridge III. "Following him as store manager was tough....Everyone loved Frank Strawbridge." Ron won them over, though, and recalls that when he left to become a divisional merchandise manager, "people cried and I cried. It was just so good." Ron's "seemingly limitless energy" and "mastery of detail" won over a lot of people and, in 1987, earned him an officer position with S&C.[192] He was promoted to VP for planning, property management and development. Although Ron, a people person, loved his new position, he admitted there was one downside to it: "The worst part of the job when I became an officer was that I didn't see anyone anymore, just the other officers and [a] few other people. I really missed the selling floor and interacting with customers."[193]

FOR ANY ASSOCIATES WHO are not represented here, please know that your time with the company was valued and appreciated. You were part of the family, and you helped make it successful.

CHAPTER 8

THE HOLIDAYS AT S&C

Merry Christmas, from our family to yours.
—1988 S&C Christmas commercial

For better or worse, without department stores, the holiday shopping season might not be what it is today. Many would argue that they could do without the pervasive commercialization and the Black Friday sales. Yet even the most disillusioned can't deny the delight and wonder they felt as a child when walking into their city's big department store during the holidays, only to be greeted with the likes of a magical winter wonderland.

A look back in time shows that gift giving and holiday festivities have been common practices in the United States since the 1600s. Not surprisingly, the Puritans attempted to outlaw Christmas celebrations, believing they were "too luxurious of a practice," but by the 1680s, they had changed their minds and permitted them.[194] It wasn't until the nineteenth century, however, that signs of commercialization appeared, thanks in large part to the Industrial Revolution and mass production of goods. The rise of the department store made gift giving more accessible to a wider population. Added to the mix was the publication of *The Night Before Christmas* by Clement Clarke Moore in 1823 and Charles Dickens's *A Christmas Carol* in 1843. Both were wildly popular and portrayed so many of the sentiments we associate with the holiday season today. December 25 became a national holiday in 1870, and by 1900, the holiday shopping season was firmly a part of the economy. In 1920, department stores escalated excitement for the holiday season with the introduction of the Thanksgiving Day parade. Philadelphia's Gimbels hosted the first Thanksgiving Day parade in the United States. It was followed in 1924 by both the Hudson Department Store parade in Detroit and the Macy's parade in New York.

Competition intensified among department stores as they competed to see which could draw the most customers with their holiday attractions and decorations. Santa was at nearly every store, patiently listening to the Christmas lists of children who lined up to sit in his lap. Shoppers treated their families to a holiday meal in festively decorated dining rooms. Carolers were heard spreading holiday cheer around the stores. Wanamaker's installed a monorail in the toy department in 1948, to the merriment of children, and started its popular light show in 1959, boasting approximately eighty thousand lights.[195] S&C also did its best to attract holiday shoppers young and old. Members of the S&C Chorus performed memorable concerts during the season at special venues in and around the city as well as for customers and employees in the Eighth and Market store. Some years, there were live nativity scenes on display in the store. Artful window displays caught the attention of people on the street. In 1923, the store introduced the Holly Girls, another idea from the productive mind of Herbert Tily. The young women dressed in holiday-inspired uniforms (sometimes red dresses with white collars) were stationed about the store to "give color to the store" while answering customer questions and guiding them to departments.[196]

Probably the most memorable S&C holiday attraction began in 1985 when the Eighth and Market store opened "A Christmas Carol." This three-dimensional animated display welcomed customers to walk through twenty-six scenes from the charming and eternally endearing book. Taking up six thousand square feet of the store on the fourth floor, the display took twenty minutes to walk through and contained over one hundred animated, three-quarter life-size figures representing characters from the book. "Each scene is dramatically heightened by antiques or authentic reproductions of furniture, cooking utensils, and household articles bringing our visitors face to face with daily life in the London of 1840."[197] As an additional attraction during its opening week, Cedric Dickens, the great-grandson of Charles Dickens, was present to autograph copies of A Christmas Carol. The display was hugely popular and saw nearly 170,000 visitors in its first six weeks.[198]

Although S&C is gone, the Dickens Village lives on at Macy's, which now occupies the old Wanamaker's building at Thirteenth and Market. It would shock Justus and Isaac to learn that their store's main holiday attraction would one day live in their archrival's location. Even more ironic is that

S&C Holly Girls, 1932. *Courtesy of the Hagley Museum and Library.*

Macy's has continued to run the old Wanamaker's light show—the upside being that Delaware Valley residents can now enjoy both holiday attractions under one roof!

Other S&C holiday traditions included a competition for students from Philadelphia's Moore College of Art to submit cover designs for the November/December issue of *Store Chat*. Started in 1964, the competition lasted until 1995. Several entries were submitted each year and voted on by Store Family Associates. In addition to having their artwork displayed on the cover of the employee magazine, winners received an S&C gift certificate.

For decades, Store Family members enjoyed gathering at the Eighth and Market Streets location early on Christmas Eve before the store opened. Surrounded by glittering holiday decorations while listening to cheerful carols sung by the S&C Chorus, employees were likely filled with anticipation and anxiety for what was in store on this last day of frantic holiday shopping. Stockton Strawbridge gave an end-of-the-year speech, a tradition he started during his presidency. Had it been a good year or a not-so-good year? That was the question on everyone's mind. The answer came at the end when he slowly lifted his pant legs to reveal: two green socks for a good year, one green and one red sock for a mixed year. Fortunately, there was never a year when two red socks were revealed. Stockton's son Peter and nephew Francis enthusiastically carried on the Christmas Eve tradition after his retirement. When recalling these holiday traditions, Francis said, "Everything was to get and keep the Store Family in a Christmas mood."[199] (Francis later told the *Philadelphia Inquirer* that he reluctantly wore two red socks to the annual executives' Christmas party in 1995, the company's last holiday season.)[200]

Keeping spirits high was necessary. November and December were the time of year when S&C, like most retailers, made its profit. Francis R. Strawbridge acknowledged that "one week in the Thanksgiving to Christmas season could equal a whole month of sales in July and August."[201] This required a dogged commitment by every employee. It was all hands on deck, from the sales floor to the warehouse to the advertising department to housekeeping to the waitstaff in the restaurants and to all the other departments and divisions that kept the store operating and the customers shopping.

Store Chat was instrumental in spreading holiday cheer, giving thanks for the hard work of all company employees while also gently encouraging their continued dedication and quality customer service in the new year. An issue from December 1911 ends with: "A Strawbridge & Clothier Resolution for the Year 1912: This YEAR, I PROMISE to treat EVERY customer with the same consideration I would wish to receive, should our positions be reversed."[202]

Members of the Strawbridge family along with S&C employees at the annual Store Family Sing, 1982. *Courtesy of the Hagley Museum and Library.*

An issue from 1906 focuses on more practical matters when asking employees to pay extra attention to sales checks during the busy shopping season and not make errors for the billing and delivery departments. Dr. Rachel Williams posted a message in the December 1944 *Store Chat* titled, "Keep Well at Christmastime: By Being a Good Tenant in a Wonderful Body." She provided health tips to help employees make it through the season, like "too many nights out make a 'toil of pleasure' instead of real relaxation" and "shoes must fit the feet and not the fancy....High heels make correct posture impossible."

A sign of changing times (and perhaps a forewarning, too) was highlighted in the November/December 1995 issue, which touted S&C's entrée into online shopping.

> *In this age of high-tech computers, S&C has left no stone unturned when it comes to reaching our target customers. Those who like to shop from their home computers can shop from Strawbridge & Clothier!*

For several years, the holiday issue of *Store Chat* contained a message from the president and chairman of the board. Stockton Strawbridge's 1961 Christmas message reflected optimism and steadfastness:

> *1962 is a fresh new year coming up, full of opportunity and challenge. It is an exciting time in which we are living: a time of growth and broadening*

horizons. Well do we realize that our strongest competitive asset for the present and the future lies in the quality and character of our fine Store Family, of whom we are so justly proud.[203]

In their 1991 message, Peter and Francis Strawbridge emphasized the hard work and dedication of Store Family members while also acknowledging signs of troubling days ahead:

As you know, 1991 has been a challenging year for Strawbridge & Clothier, as well as the entire retail industry. The holiday selling period is an important one for us, one that requires a high degree of diligence and determination. You have demonstrated these qualities in the past, so we are confident that your continued efforts and enthusiasm will greatly contribute to our success this year, and help us face head-on the challenges of 1992.[204]

These warnings continued to be a theme until their last message in 1995.

HOLIDAY SEASON MEMORIES

The Dickens Display was second to none and was an instant classic.... It was always very busy. The people were usually very nice except for the closing hours on Christmas Eve, when panic would set in.
—*Ray Pascali, S&C Sales Associate, 1979–84*[205]

Working on the floor was great. Starting with November Clover. I can remember the sound of people running into the store on that Saturday morning at 801 Market and I was on the second floor....I was a full-time stock person, and Mr. Miller hired me to manage the gift certificate booths in the Philadelphia store. I worked every day, seven days a week, from Black Friday to Christmas Eve.
—*Michael Dailey, stock 1978–81, receiving manager, 1981–86*[206]

My very favorite memory was entering through the Filbert Street doors before the store was open for the day on cold winter days (I walked to work in those days) and the wonderful smells of the Food Hall.
—*Susan Sander, manager of the Dickens attraction and special events coordinator, 1985–97*[207]

It was always a fun and festive atmosphere. I remember one of the Strawbridges coming around to wish everyone a happy holiday and then we could leave.
—*Nancy O'Donnell Abbot, communications coordinator, 1983–87*[208]

It was magical. Everyone was happy and nice, for the most part. I remember one Christmas Eve and gift wrap was short of help, so they sent a bunch of department managers to help gift wrap. If you remember, those wrappings were very intricate, and we did our best to try to get the packages to match the samples. Some looked pretty sad.
—*Michele O'Connell, divisional sales manager, food services, 1973–96*[209]

I remember being so excited to go to work on Black Friday because we would get to see the beautiful decorations and listen to the beautiful Christmas music....Our Christmases were always filled with those beautiful yellow boxes. I also loved the Christmas festivities, especially the Christmas carols and the speech from one of the Strawbridges and the revealing of the Christmas socks he wore.
—*Danielle Leon Speiser, merchandise information operations department, 1989–96*[210]

S&C's Santas

While a student at St. Joseph's University, Kevin Neary landed the job of Santa in 1983 as a way to earn some extra money during the holidays. Thirteen years later, he was still the S&C Santa, even after moving to Florida. Until the last holiday season at S&C in 1995, Kevin made the trip back to Philadelphia to don his red suit and white beard and charm and be charmed by countless children. "Thank goodness for Strawbridge & Clothier. Children have lost a certain sense of Santa over the years....We all grew up with the basic concept that Santa visits a Department Store, not the mall."[211]

HOLIDAY CUSTOMER CARE

In 1986, Deborah Faragher was walking through the television department at the Plymouth Meeting store, of which she was now the manager after previously managing the Ardmore store. She came across an older man, Mr. Hirshberger, who, as she described, looked forlorn. He had lost his wife that year and was trying to do the Christmas shopping for his grandchildren but didn't know how to start, since his wife had typically done the shopping. Deborah offered her assistance and helped him find what he needed. So appreciative was Mr. Hirshberger that he wrote a letter to Stockton Strawbridge, who was chairman of the board's executive committee at the time. Stockton responded to the letter and wrote a letter of appreciation to Deborah. Mr. Hirshberger returned for the next two Christmases, and each time, Deborah assisted him. At one point, they even enjoyed lunch together following his shopping. Mr. Hirshberger sent more letters of thanks to Stockton, and Stockton wrote more letters of appreciation to Deborah. In 1988, he finally wrote to Deborah that he would soon be clearing out his office at S&C to make room for Deborah's inevitable occupation of it:

> It would appear to me that Mr. Hirshberger is going to place your name before the Board for—at the very least—Chairmanship of the Executive Committee, our first female Chairperson to be elected in that capacity.

Stockton ended the letter with his endorsement.[212]

HOLIDAY INCLUSION

A month of nonstop Christmas-themed festivities and traditions raises the question: What was it like for employees who did not celebrate Christmas? When asked if the company in some way recognized its employees of different faiths during the holiday season, Steven L. Strawbridge said they did not. "I am afraid the Company had very little social awareness (on such issues) back in the 1980s or 1990s."[213] S&C was not alone; most retailers did not. Although retailers began to move away from advertising with "Merry Christmas" to "Happy Holidays" in the 1990s, the focus was likely more on customers of different faiths than on employees.

For Betsy Horen, S&C's handbag buyer and a practicing Jew, the holiday season was always the highlight of the year for her.

My gentile friends would always laugh at me, as I ran out of my office on the top of the balcony, in the Food Hall, to make sure that I got a good spot to be able to listen to all of the holiday speeches…and join in on any Christmas songs that would be sung that morning before the store opened.…

I never felt that major Jewish holidays were acknowledged, but then there was not an overflowing of Jewish employees working for S&C.…Please know that even though I felt that my three major Jewish holidays were never acknowledged, I never felt uncomfortable. I always took Rosh Hashanah and Yom Kippur off to be able to go to synagogue to pray.[214]

CHAPTER 9

LOVE AND MARRIAGE

A Selection of S&C and Clover Romances

DAWN DOWNEY BUNDICK was working in Men's Underwear and Pajamas at Eighth and Market in the summer of 1989 when her sister told her she had met the perfect guy for her. Her sister, who worked in the Machine Shop, introduced Dawn to Marc, who worked in MIO (Merchandise Information Operations) installing the new system to allow merchandise to be scanned with a UPC code. Not long after, Marc began working in Dawn's department. "I found myself more eager than normal to get to work in the mornings," she recalled. The two started dating in July 1989 and were engaged in 1992. "We totally felt the S&C family love during our engagement as we ended up having three showers from our different departments." As spouses and, later, parents, Marc and Dawn continued growing their careers at S&C. Dawn became a department manager and Marc worked for the help desk. "We cried that day in '96 when we all heard the news that we were selling, but we had to smile for what S&C brought into our lives. It will always be a part of our story."[215]

GEORGE DIEM was working as a vertical and diagonal transportation engineer for S&C when he met and fell in love with Lillie Hansel, an elevator operator, in 1964.

JIM HANLEY AND SARAH OSKI HANLEY met and fell in love while attending Drexel University in the early 1980s. Both found part-time work at S&C

while in college. On graduating with a degree in accounting, Jim tried his hand at the profession for a year, only to find it didn't suit him. He returned to retail in 1983 and applied for a job in the Clover discount division. Both Jim and Sarah entered the Executive Development Program, Jim for Clover and Sarah for S&C. Although most classes were separated by division, students would sometimes get to attend special sessions together and enjoyed a joint graduation ceremony. Married in 1984, the two developed a reputation as one of the few cross-divisional couples in the company.

Jim and Sarah often swapped stories about their day and joked about the differences between the divisions. Jim acknowledged that although Clover was a great place to work, it didn't have the style of S&C. It wasn't uncommon for Sarah to ask sarcastically at the end of a workday, "Did you put out enough paper towels today?" or "How did those lunch kits do?" She was selling brands like Jordache jeans and Ralph Lauren. Retail hours weren't easy for the newlyweds. Jim joked that they never saw each other at Christmas. Throughout the year, they did their best to make sure they had at least one day off together and that they spent their mornings together when they worked later hours. "You're as supportive as can be, and you work together as much as you can," he said.

Sarah left S&C after a couple of years to pursue a career in marketing. Jim remained with Clover for ten years, eventually becoming the store manager of the Ralph's Corner branch store. When he accepted a job with another retailer in September 1993, he remembers receiving a phone call from Peter Strawbridge a couple of days before he left. Peter called to thank him. "He was incredibly gracious and thanked me for my time.…I miss the stores. I love the fact that the family was the family and not just the people who had their name on the door," said Jim.[216]

MICHAEL DRYSDALE worked in personnel for the Clover division in the mid-1970s. "Fond of snow skiing," he was asked by Bob Malloy to coordinate a ski trip for Clover employees, in conjunction with the annual S&C ski trip. "In this way, I met Grace Olson, who worked for Bob. Sometimes Grace's daughter Carol would join her for lunch at Eighth and Market. When Carol graduated college in 1980, she was hired by the tour broker that handled the ski trip. Meanwhile, I had been moonlighting on weekends for Adventure Unlimited for ski trips. It was only natural that I would see Carol Olson regularly. One thing led to another. Carol and I have been married since 1984."[217]

PAUL GREENHOLT was attending the University of Delaware in 1985 when he transferred from the Concord branch store to the Christiana store to work as the night regular in Young Men's. "So the week that I transferred, the manager was introducing me around the department, including [to] the lovely and talented Susan Loebe. I was smitten. A few months later, we began dating.…We were engaged in 1987 and married in 1988. We have been married now for thirty-four years."[218]

MICHELE O'CONNELL met her husband at the Strawbridge & Clothier bowling league in Cherry Hill. "We got to spend every Thursday night at the bowling alley until [February] when we realized there was something more there. We've been married almost 34 years."[219]

RAY PASCALI says:

> I first met my wife Diane Boyko Pascali in August of 1984 during the closeout sale of the Wilmington store. We each volunteered for the closeout sale to earn some extra money. After the sale had ended, we would occasionally see each other on the Frankford El platform going home. We both lived in Northeast Philadelphia. At the time, I wasn't interested in dating anyone so I tried to avoid her. I later learned that she would sometimes let the first train pass so we could ride home together. Her persistence prevailed. When we worked evenings, we would see each other in the store and eventually tried to schedule our breaks together. One day a co-worker said to me, "That girl on the 8th floor really likes you, you should ask her out on a date." The next day I went into the electronics offices behind the 5th floor TV department and called her to see if she would be interested in going to a Flyers hockey game with me. I was so nervous after she accepted that I said, "I will pick me up at six," when I meant to say, "I will pick you up at six."
>
> We dated for the next six years and were engaged to be married on Christmas Eve, December 24, 1988. We were married September 15, 1990. If I could do it over again, I would have proposed on the 1st floor of the Center City store at 8th and Market streets.[220]

ROBERT PHILLIPS says:

> I met my wife, Theresa Jumper (Phillips) at Clover while preparing to open the Palmer Park Mall store #17 in 1982. She was divorced with three children and I was single and 10 years younger than her. She was a

department manager and I was a new hire at Palmer as an assistant dept. manager. It was rumored when we first got together that Clover instituted its "no fraternization" policy because of us. There were times when she was serving as the manager-on-duty which meant that she would be my supervisor, certainly a conflict. The policy was implemented not long after we "came out" as a couple. She was promoted to assistant store manager in #16 Whitehall which resolved the problem. We went on to be married in 1983. We both worked for Clover until it was closed in 1996.

Theresa passed away in June 2021. She left me with 5 children and 9 grandchildren all of which are happy and very close as families go. I could write a novel or a romance about our almost 40-year life together which would not have happened were it not for us meeting at Clover all of those years ago. [221]

Francis R. Strawbridge III says:

I was the Store Manager of our Springfield branch store and Mary Jo Beatty was the Department Manager of our Accessories Department. The Accessories Department was at the foot of the escalator on the middle level of the Springfield store and I kept passing that Department (and Mary Jo) on my frequent walking trips through the Store. My trips and our conversations became more frequent and longer. We dated after one of our Springfield Store Anniversary Sale rallies and the dates grew more frequent. We were married within the year. That was in 1969. [222]

CHAPTER 10

RESPONDING TO

CHANGING TIMES

S&C began its story in one century and ended it in another. The 128 years in between saw technological innovations that forever changed the way Americans live, work and consume, as well as social and political events that changed the way Americans see their world. The American department store provided a stage for some of these key events to play out.

War Years

When the United States joined the Allied Powers during World War I in 1917, S&C saw 256 of its approximately 5,000 employees either enlist or accept conscription into the armed services.[223] Many of the remaining employees supported the war effort through Liberty Loan drives that the company conducted at its Eighth and Market Streets store. Across the nation, the loss of warehouse workers to the war impacted production levels, resulting in low merchandise and diminished surplus stock for retailers. Department store executives formed the National War Service Committee in 1918 to decide on ways to ease some of the pain felt by the industry. S&C's Herbert Tily was elected as the chairman, and under him, the committee agreed on ways to rein in expenses and promote sales. This included limiting home deliveries and encouraging shoppers to take their purchases with them (most Americans still did not own cars, so it was common to have purchases delivered). The Christmas shopping season was also extended to October, giving shoppers plenty of time to benefit from sales.

World War I coincided with S&C's golden anniversary. Despite labor and stock shortages, S&C managed to successfully celebrate its fifty years and held special sales in January and June 1918.

When World War I finally ended on Armistice Day in 1918, Alfred Lief writes, S&C invited the Store Family to attend an eleven o'clock thanksgiving service in the store's auditorium and closed for business for the rest of the day.[224] In 1919, the company unveiled a large bronze tablet it had commissioned with the names of all 260 men from S&C who ultimately served in the war, five of whom lost their lives. The tablet still hangs on a wall on the first floor mezzanine.[225]

Just twenty-five years later, the company faced labor and material shortages again when the United States entered World War II in 1942. This time, 373 employees left their jobs at S&C to serve in the armed forces.[226] As a sendoff, they received the equivalent of their summer vacation pay. Despite wartime disruptions to manufacturing and the delivery of goods, the company tried to maintain its honest relationship with customers, advertising when merchandise was of "inferior quality." The operating board instructed that such merchandise at Eighth and Market be sold in the basement, the store's discount department. Home deliveries were reduced once more due to gas rationing and government restrictions on rubber, which had to be conserved for tanks. Customers were given free shopping bags to encourage them to take their purchases home with them. For those deliveries that were made, delivery truck drivers could not go more than thirty-five miles an hour.

The Store Family demonstrated wide support for the war effort. Along with in-store war bond drives, employee blood drives were held. The Ardmore store formed a Sunshine Club to send care packages to its employees who left for the service. S&C's Candy Department shipped candy to employees fighting abroad as well as to the loved ones of S&C employees who left to fight. The Jenkintown store worked with the National Farm School to create a demo victory garden, which the store displayed. *Store Chat* resumed publication after its Depression-era hiatus and was mailed to S&C employees in service to keep their Store Family ties strong. Starting in May 1944, S&C worked with Philadelphia's evening newspaper, the *Philadelphia Bulletin*, to produce a weekly edition that was sent to employees in the service and given to customers to mail overseas. In addition to staying on top of Philadelphia news and events, soldiers could read personal messages that were written in a blank space on the back page. When publication of the weekly ceased in 1946, seven million copies had been mailed to soldiers.[227] The Eighth and Market Streets store welcomed the navy to set up a recruiting station in one of the windows facing Market Street. The Women's Army Corps (WAC), which formed in response to Pearl Harbor, also shared the space. The station successfully attracted customers, passersby and S&C employees alike. The Philadelphia chapter of the WAC Mothers Club was allowed to meet once a month in the store's exhibition space.[228] The company also continued its charitable contributions to the Red Cross, the Salvation Army, the United War Chest and the American Friends Service Committee, among others.

After World War II, two tablets with the names of S&C employees who served were placed in the first-floor elevator cross lobby. They bore the names of 373 men and women, 8 of whom lost their lives.[229]

After World War I, S&C adopted what would become a long-standing Veterans Day tradition. S&C employees and customers were welcome to participate in the observance held at the Eighth and Market store. S&C officer Frank Veale eloquently describes the moving ceremony in his book *Family Business: Strawbridge & Clothier: The Momentous Seventies*:

Just as World War I coincided with S&C's fiftieth anniversary, the company's seventy-fifth anniversary fell during World War II, in 1943. Instead of celebrating with an anniversary sale, as it had done in 1918, the company decided to hold a special sale for war bonds and stamps, to serve as an extra push for the war bond drives already in place. Customers and employees were welcome to admire Norman Rockwell's Four Freedoms paintings, which were displayed at the celebration before they began a tour of other cities.[*]

---

[*] Lief, *Family Business*, 228.

> *Beginning with a quiet hymn from our Glee Club, followed by a message of tribute, the reading of the roll-call of our company's war dead (for many years spoken by Isaac Clothier, Jr. in his inimitably emotional manner), punctuated by the soft litany of the singers, and ending with a silence and a playing of taps followed by the haunting sound of a faintly echoing bugle in the distance, this ceremony rarely failed to move its combined audience of customers and fellow workers alike.[230]*

The Veterans Day ceremony came to an end in 1970. Responding to the divisive emotions that seized the country during the Vietnam War, the company switched to a scaled-back observance in which Eighth and Market and all S&C branch stores announced a moment of silence and the playing of taps. This observance continued until 1996.

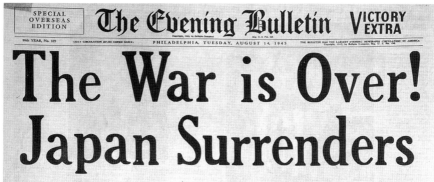

SPECIAL OVERSEAS EDITION

The Evening Bulletin

VICTORY EXTRA

99th YEAR, No. 105   (JULY CIRCULATION 467,945 COPIES DAILY)   PHILADELPHIA, TUESDAY, AUGUST 14, 1945   THE BULLETIN HAS THE LARGEST EVENING NEWSPAPER CIRCULATION IN AMERICA

The War is Over!
Japan Surrenders

THRONGS GO WILD ALL OVER CITY AT WORD OF PEACE

Snake-Dance in Central Streets as Mighty Roar Greets War's End

Philadelphia, on edge to celebrate final victory, cut loose with a terrific burst of enthusiasm when word spread shortly after 7 P. M. that the Japs officially had quit.

Throwing reserve to the winds, they whooped and hollered, snake danced through the streets to the accompaniment of an ear-splitting din set up by automobile horns, whistles and horns.

It was a moment for which they had been waiting all day. A day in which their emotions went up and down like the tides, depending on the news from Washington on the progress of the Japanese answer.

Crowds in the downtown sections which had gathered throughout the day lost no time in giving voice to their approval to the end of the war.

They lost no time surging into Market and Chestnut sts., writhing like a huge snake up and down the middle of the thoroughfares. There was no doubt left in anyone's mind as to the authenticity of the announcement when the sirens on City Hall cut loose at 7.05 P. M. Their wail brought fresh bursts of approval from the holiday-like crowds.

The sounding of the sirens was preceded by an Evening Bulletin Flashcast announcement saying simply: "It's official." This started a long gasp from those nearby, to be followed by a mighty roar with all stops out. Ticker tape cascaded from surrounding buildings.

Policemen made no attempt to curb the activities of the merrymakers. Hugging and kissing was the rule rather than the exception, and American flags suddenly appeared like magic among the throng.

THIS OVERSEAS EDITION

Especially Prepared for

The Men and Women of the

U. S. Armed Services

Compliments of

Strawbridge & Clothier

Killed by Train

MRS. BEATRICE VARE SHAW

MRS. SHAW'S DEATH BY TRAIN PROBED

Daughter of the late Wm. S. Vare was Killed near Haverford Station

An investigation of the circumstances under which Mrs. Beatrice Vare Shaw, daughter of the late William S. Vare, was killed by a fast Pennsylvania Railroad train at the Haverford Station Sunday, was begun by Montgomery County Coroner W. J. Rushong.

Pending completion of his investigation, Coroner Rushong said he was withholding a death certificate.

The body of Mrs. Shaw, who was the widow of Dr. John J. Shaw, her father's personal physician and former State Secretary of Health, was found about 200 feet east of the station platform after a train passed.

Police of Lower Merion Township said they had been unable to find anyone who saw the accident although several neighbors said they had observed her walking toward the station from her home at 260 Cheswold lane.

Police said there was a possibility she had tried to cross the tracks unaware of the train's approach.

Mrs. Shaw, who was 42, early became her father's confidante and served as his private secretary for a number of years. When he was stricken with paralysis several years before his death, she acted as liaison officer between her father and his political lieutenants here.

STORES CLOSE TOMORROW

Philadelphia's central city stores will be closed tomorrow in observance of the Japanese surrender.

The city's municipal celebration of victory at Independence Hall will be held until President Truman announces Allied and Japanese signing of the terms.

Tojo Effigy to be Burned at Bonfire here Tonight

Police and firemen, the premier who headed Japan's war lords during her period of conquest, will be burned in effigy this evening on 28th st. near Huntington.

Residents of the neighborhood feed the time for the big bonfire at early evening, although a little one—sort of a warning to Tojo of what is to come—was burned beneath the effigy early today.

The dummy Tojo—a pair of old gray trousers, a stuffed brown shirt, and hay-filled white sugar bag to form a face—hung like a scarecrow from a light standard.

21,749 CASUALTIES FROM THIS AREA

War Toll will be more when Untabulated Names Come in

The recorded cost of the war in casualties to the Philadelphia area stood today at 21,749 killed, missing, wounded and prisoner.

This figure includes casualties announced today by the services, but is one that is bound to be increased by casualties that have not yet been listed.

During the first 14 days of August announced casualties for the city were 139, bringing the total since Pearl Harbor to 15,078. For the adjacent area, the nearby portions of Delaware, Montgomery, Camden, Chester, and Bucks Counties during the same period 72 casualties were announced, bringing their total since the war to 6,670.

In Philadelphia, the August totals to date were 32 killed, five missing, 102 wounded and none taken prisoner, bringing the totals since Pearl Harbor to 3,436 killed, 1,527 missing, 1,693 wounded, and 1,492 prisoners.

Allied Ruler of Japan

General of the Army DOUGLAS MacARTHUR

CAPS MADE IN JAPAN SOLD ON STREETS

Hundreds of persons celebrated V-J Day prematurely today, and perhaps unknowingly, with cheap, thin, colored cardboard caps — caps that were made in Japan.

Street vendors, with an eye on more for the 25 cents the caps brought than for patriotism, scratched out the "made-in-Japan" stamp in some instances, but many sold them brazenly with the notation untouched.

The caps, leftovers from the New York World's Fair in 1933, were blue and gold with peak and imitation feather.

SIRENS BLOW ENCORE— AT MAYOR'S REQUEST

Mayor Samuel gave vent to his own V-J Day feeling this evening by blowing the air raid sirens atop City Hall twice as long as was planned.

After operating the lever which controls the mechanism the prescribed number of times—six blasts of 30 seconds each—he turned to two Electrical Bureau employes who were timing the blasts in Room 620 and said:

"Don't you think the occasion calls for a repeat performance? I think the public deserves it."

With that he launched a second series of blasts.

HOLIDAY FOR CITY WORKERS

Mayor Samuel this evening said that all city employes would be given a day off tomorrow to celebrate the coming of peace.

In a happy mood, the Mayor wore a broad grin as he left City Hall around 8 o'clock.

It was announced the holiday would apply to all persons on the city payroll, exclusive of the police and firemen, and key persons needed to keep essential facilities going.

CITY TAPROOMS CLOSED ON MARTIN'S ORDER

Police, at 8 P. M., were ordered by Superintendent Sutton to close all taprooms and places dispensing alcoholic beverages in compliance with Governor Martin's order.

In the hour between the announcement of the Jap surrender and issuance of the order, taprooms were jammed, people stood three and four deep at the bars, and police and some difficulty in emptying many of them.

The Governor said the action was taken out of respect for the more than 20,000 Pennsylvania boys and girls who have made the supreme sacrifice, and their families.

By The Associated Press

Washington, Aug. 14—President Truman announced at 7:00 P. M. unqualified Japanese acceptance of surrender terms. The war is over.

The surrender will be accepted by General Douglas MacArthur when arrangements can be made.

Mr. Truman read the formal message relayed from Emperor Hirohito through the Swiss Government in which the Japanese ruler pledged the surrender on the terms laid down by the Big 3 conference at Potsdam.

President Truman made this statement:

"I have received this afternoon a message from the Japanese Government in reply to the message forwarded to that Government by the Secretary of State on August 11.

"I deem this reply a full acceptance of the Potsdam declaration which specifies the unconditional surrender of Japan.

"In this reply there is no qualification.

"Arrangements are now being made for the formal signing of surrender terms at the earliest possible moment.

"General Douglas MacArthur has been appointed the supreme Allied Commander to receive the Japanese surrender.

"Great Britain, Russia and China will be represented by high ranking officers.

"Meantime, the Allied armed forces have been ordered to suspend offensive action.

"The proclamation of V-J Day must wait upon the formal signing of the surrender terms by Japan."

The White House made public the Japanese Government's message ending the war which started December 7, 1941.

'Shamed Japs Bow to Very Ground'

The final decision had been heralded by a Domei broadcast that "on August 14, 1945," the Imperial decision was granted" and that weeping people had gathered before the Emperor's palace and "bowed to the very ground" in their shame that their "efforts were not enough."

The portion of the Domei despatch on the Emperor's decision said Hirohito had felt "extreme concern" ever since his rescript of December 8, 1941, with which he declared war.

As recorded and translated by FCC, the despatch read:

"How shall the 100,000,000 people, filled with trepidation, reply to the Emperor? His Majesty's subjects are moved to tears by His Majesty's boundless and infinite solicitude.

"August 14, 1945, the Imperial decision was granted. The palace grounds are quiet beneath the dark clouds.

"Honored with the Imperial edict in the sublime palace grounds, the mob of loyal people are bowed to the very ground in front of the Niju-Bashi (the bridge which leads to the palace.)

"Their tears flow unchecked. Alas! In their shame, how can the people raise their heads?"

Overseas edition of the *Evening Bulletin* sponsored by Strawbridge & Clothier. *Courtesy of the Hagley Museum and Library.*

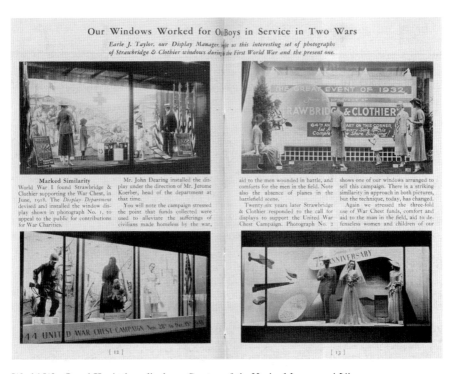

World War I and II window displays. *Courtesy of the Hagley Museum and Library.*

Left: Opening ceremony for the storewide Third War Loan Rally. *Courtesy of the Hagley Museum and Library.*

Right: WAC recruiting office window display. *Courtesy of the Hagley Museum and Library.*

One of the last Veteran's Day observances at Eighth and Market store. *Courtesy of the Hagley Museum and Library.*

THE DEPRESSION YEARS

Alfred Lief writes that 1929 was supposed to be a "banner year" for S&C. Construction of the new store at Eighth and Market started in January, and excitement was in the air about the architectural marvel. By October, that excitement had turned to grave concern with the stock market crash. Plans went ahead, however, for the new store, which was successfully completed in 1932. Still, the financial strains of the 1930s left their mark on S&C.

The decade would be a roller-coaster ride of rising and declining sales. Higher state and federal taxes ate away at much of the company's gross profits. Sales from the Ardmore and Jenkintown branch stores, though good, were not enough to overcome the declines at Eighth and Market. Cost-saving practices were necessary. Starting in 1932, dividends ceased on the company's preferred and common stock. Officers took a salary cut, the basic wage was reduced and overtime payment ceased.[231] There would no longer be elevator attendants to assist the operators with opening the doors. Instead, longer handles were installed for the operators. Merchandise stock was reduced. *Store Chat* was suspended, and the advertising budget was reduced. The employee pension fund, Relief Association and savings fund were all impacted, since they had relied on dividends from their shares of preferred stock to supplement member dues and the company's annual financial contributions. In order to keep the funds afloat, the company continued making its annual contributions and bought the preferred stock shares the funds owned. Since the value of the shares had decreased, the company also made up the cost difference.[232] Despite cuts, S&C did not discontinue its charitable donations. It continued to contribute to area colleges, hospitals and a citywide campaign for the relief of the unemployed.

S&C recognized that now more than ever, customers needed to be reassured of the store's quality and trustworthy customer service. Isaac Clothier Jr. said as much when speaking to employees during a lecture on merchandising: "The firm realizes that respect cannot be gained or held without a strict adherence to the Golden Rule."[233] In order to keep patronage stable during such difficult times, the company was willing to make certain investments in its employees. Training became increasingly important, leading to the creation of the Executive Development Program (which really took off under Stockton in the 1950s). Employees like Ella Waters were allowed to experiment with new attractions like the in-store fashion show. The Staff Council was created to improve communication between employees and executives. All these practices would bind employees closer to the company, maintain its customer base and help S&C weather the storm.

WOMEN AND RETAIL

One could argue that department stores would not have had their golden age without women, thanks not only to the purchasing power of "Mrs. Consumer" but also to the throngs of women who stood behind the sales counters and kept the customers coming back. It should not be surprising, then, that with this new sense of economic independence and market influence, these women also experienced a political awakening.

Signs of this awakening emerged in the early teens with the advocacy work around a minimum wage for women. Typically opposed to government regulation, department store executives, surprisingly, embraced this Progressive-era movement. "Merchants bent their thinking on the relationship between business and government policy in part to conciliate middle-class white women shoppers who were their most important market and who were increasingly influenced by prominent women reformers and consumer organizations."[234] Merchants were also determined to perform damage control after a string of scarring reports and publications that accused them of paying women workers low wages and permitting "immoral contacts" between saleswomen and male shoppers. It was believed that, in some cases, poor working conditions "pushed saleswomen into prostitution."[235] Criticism was also directed at the lack of adequate breaks for women to rest their tired feet after standing for hours upon hours. White lists were issued by the National Consumers' League to help shoppers determine which stores were deemed fair employers.

To protect their image, department stores began implementing their own reform efforts, like more employee training opportunities, nicer lunchrooms and cleaner locker rooms. Retail historian Vicki Howard describes how these voluntary changes "emphasized the importance of salespeople to the image of the store and the success of the business." Stores hoped this would "reclaim the faith of women customers who shopped with the latest 'whitelist' in hand."[236] Although it is not clear if S&C supported a minimum wage for women (or if it was included on the local white list), the store did make its own voluntary changes by creating an employee lounge and lunchroom for its female workers during the early 1900s.

Massachusetts passed the nation's first minimum wage law in 1912. It was limited to women and children, who made up the majority of workers in the state's mills and factories. Over the next two decades, more states would adopt minimum wage laws affecting both men and women. The Fair Labor Standards Act of 1938 established the first federal minimum wage.*

The push for better working conditions and wages coincided with the growing suffragist movement in the United States. Many department stores wanted to display their support to stay in the good graces of their female customers. Some targeted their advertising to suffragette sympathizers

---

* Patrick J. Kiger, "Minimum Wage in America: A Timeline," History.com, last modified October 28, 2019, https://www.history.com/news/minimum-wage-america-timeline.

and even allowed suffragettes to use their street-front windows to display pamphlets and other materials.[237] As with the general population, there were presumably Store Family members who were in favor of and opposed to the suffragist cause. Scholar Jerome Bjelopera found a *Store Chat* issue that contained a review of a 1912 minstrel show performance by S&C's all-female Clover Mandolin club called the "Women's Suffrage Parade." Bjelopera suggests that, along with resorting to racist impressions for entertainment value, the show displayed anti-suffragette sentiment by portraying women's rights activists as "overly aggressive" and "anti-masculine."[238] Whatever the predominant opinion was among S&C employees, once the Nineteenth Amendment passed, the company demonstrated its support by printing voter instruction leaflets for the Pennsylvania League of Women Voters.[239]

Despite these progressive steps, gender equality remained very much a work in progress in the retail industry. Like most department stores, women were mainly found on S&C's sales floor but not as much in its executive and corporate offices. By the middle of the twentieth century, more women were filling executive-level positions such as buyer, divisional merchandise manager and branch store manager. The gains were few and far between, however. In 1944, Rosalie E. Romeyn became the first woman store manager when she was promoted to acting manager of the Jenkintown store.[240] Yet it wasn't until nearly thirty years later, in 1977, that a woman was again promoted to store manager: Deborah Faragher of the Ardmore store.

Leonard Shea, who worked in personnel for S&C from 1962 to 1972 and later became the VP for personnel and services for the Clover division, recalls discriminatory hiring practices in his early personnel days. "Women were frequently disqualified for having a 'mass in the abdomen.' Women

were typically paid ten cents per hour less than men, and we were discouraged from hiring women from Roman Catholic colleges as it was assumed they would soon marry and become pregnant." He remembers that job stereotypes started to change with the Vietnam War. "The draft severely limited the supply of young men, and we found that many of those jobs, particularly in merchandise handling could be adequately performed by women."[241]

It wasn't until 1976 that the company had its first woman vice president, Natalie Weintraub, who was promoted to VP of general

Natalie Weintraub. *Courtesy of the author.*

Nancy Longstreth and Margaret Clews. *Courtesy of the author.*

merchandise for S&C. Progress remained slow, though; out of eighteen corporate officers in 1996, only two were women: Thelma A. Newman, VP and general merchandise manager for S&C, and Alice T. Kanigowski, VP and general merchandise manager for Clover.[242] Although several S&C employees interviewed recall more and more women filling executive-level positions during the 1980s and '90s, data cannot be provided, since the company did not formally track employee demographics.

According to Leonard Shea, S&C's in-store physician was so conservative that he never used the word *pregnant*, preferring *mass in the abdomen* instead.

Francis R. Strawbridge estimates that nearly half of all buyers for the company were women in 1996. Leonard Shea voluntarily tracked demographic data for certain Clover employees. His notes show that in 1996, nine out of twenty-seven Clover store managers were women, and six out of twenty-one divisional managers were women.

In 1984, the company finally had female representation on its thirteen-person board of directors, electing Nancy Longstreth and Margaret S. Clews. According to Francis R. Strawbridge, the year 1984 saw a push to have more women enter the boardrooms of corporate America.

Francis said that Nancy and Margaret, as descendants of Justus Strawbridge, were a perfect fit, "adding new family members to an already family-dominated board."[243] S&C would go on to elect two more women to its board in 1994: Natalie Weintraub (who had recently retired) and Jennifer Gorman-Strawbridge, one of Peter's daughters. Perhaps this was a sign of growing momentum. Had S&C remained in business in the twenty-first century and with a new generation at the helm, there may have been many more women executives, corporate officers and board members.

Retail remains a popular employment option for women, who make up the vast majority of the industry's salesforce. Men continue to hold most top executive positions. There are signs of progress, however. In 2021, ten of the forty-one female CEOs of Fortune 500 companies were in retail.*

---

* Lauren Thomas, "The Retail Industry Is Leading the Way as Women Take Over CEO Roles," CNBC, December 28, 2020, https://www.cnbc.com/2020/12/28/the-retail-industry-is-leading-the-way-as-women-take-over-ceo-roles.html.

ARDMORE'S WOMAN MANAGER

Deborah Faragher. *Courtesy of Deborah Faragher.*

When Deborah Faragher was four years old, her father passed away, leaving her mother with two children to raise on her own. Although Deborah's mother was a registered nurse, she was not employed at the time of her husband's death. Money being tight, she took it on herself to let creditors know that she would be late with her payments. According to Deborah, her mother went to the credit departments of certain department stores in Center City Philadelphia and left feeling humiliated. At S&C, however, Deborah said her mother was treated with compassion. She was taken to the uniform department, where she could pick out what she needed to return to work as a nurse and was told to "pay as she could." Little did her mother know that this would be the beginning of a long-term relationship between S&C and her family.

Nearly two decades later, in 1966, Deborah found herself working in S&C's Millinery Department as part of Drexel University's Retail Co-op Program. Once she graduated from Drexel in 1969, she became an assistant buyer, and in less than three years, she was promoted to buyer. She had always enjoyed fashion and the glamor of department stores, so this seemed like a great career fit. However, the longer she was at S&C, the more interested she became in the broader management aspects of the company, unlike many of her female colleagues, who were focused on merchandising. At the age of twenty-three, she became the merchandise manager at the Plymouth Meeting branch store. After proving herself in this position, she decided to apply for the position of store manager when she got wind that Ralph Walker was retiring as store manager of Ardmore. To her surprise, she was promoted. She was only twenty-seven. When asked how she felt about being the first woman manager of the Ardmore store and at such a young age, she admitted she was anxious but excited: "But it gave me confidence that the company put its trust in me to manage the Ardmore store."

Deborah recalls that when she first started her new job, she experienced some pushback from a few employees who weren't ready for change: "Who is this young woman coming in and telling me how to do my job?" For the most part, though, there was no resistance. She quickly gained the support of her staff by working alongside them and never asking anyone to do something she wouldn't do. "I wanted to not only lead them but develop them so they could be more fulfilled in their job and more successful," she said.

For nine years, Deborah was the only woman store manager, but then, in the 1980s, "It was like the floodgates opened." Many women were promoted to store manager. Deborah said the same was true for women as divisional merchandise managers. In 1986, Deborah went on to be store manager of Plymouth Meeting and, finally, Cherry Hill, where she ended her long career with S&C in 1996.[244]

WOMEN VOICES OF S&C

Sandra Jackson

Since there was no maternity leave in 1970, Sandra Jackson had to resign as a proofreader in the Advertising Department when she became pregnant. In 1971, after an associate was promoted, Sandra was rehired. She soon found herself juggling a demanding job and raising two young children. Trying to work around her children's daycare schedule, she would arrive at work half an hour early. One time, daycare ended at five o'clock instead of five thirty. S&C had no flextime then. Knowing she would be docked thirty minutes when clocking out even though she had arrived early, a fellow female copywriter offered to clock her out at five thirty. "That's a favor I've always appreciated. Women have always been really sly when dealing with men who are in charge," Sandra recalled.[245]

Natalie Weintraub

Natalie Weintraub, S&C's only female VP for several years, has fond memories of her time with the company. "I loved my job. I loved the people." She felt supported by her male colleagues and learned a lot from her supervisor while a buyer. Starting out as a young woman along with Peter and Francis Strawbridge, Natalie described how she "grew up" with them. She always joined the men for lunch, either in the Corinthian Room or out in town. "We had a lot of fun."[246]

Deborah Faragher

"In 1973, an invitation to the executive picnic was sent. The invitation said, 'To All Executives,' but it was only sent to the men." Deborah recalls how she and fifteen or twenty other women, mainly buyers and assistants who worked under Natalie Weintraub and Ken Brownell, decided to picket the event, which was held at Haverford College. They asked

Boys and Girls Together at Executive Outing

Photos taken by R. B. Dallas, Executive Development Director, show outcome of change in plans for the annual executive outings. The August 23 outing at Haverford College drew 105 Associates, the largest attendance on record. A good time was had by all.

MARY Flaherty, Better Dresses buyer, and Anne Stein

STOCKTON Strawbridge and Anne Stein, Wig Salon

BATTER UP—F. R. Strawbridge, III, DMM, and Elaine Foley, Supervisor, Sales Audit, Clover.

REFRESHMENT Time.

TALKING IT OVER—G. L. Cullen, Vice President for Personnel, and a trio of young executives—Debbie Kennedy, left, Young Jr. Sportswear buyer; Debbie Laverell, Springfield Manager, Sportswear; Linda Lauer, Better Jr. Sportswear buyer.

TENNIS COURT ACTION—Nick Eggleston, Casual Coats buyer, and Natalie Weintraub, DMM.

Opposite: Picket signs at the July executive outing in 1973. *Courtesy of the Hagley Museum and Library.*

Above: The August executive outing welcomed men and women. *Courtesy of the Hagley Museum and Library.*

159

women in advertising to write jingles for them, made signs with slogans and wore T-shirts that read, "KB's Babies." When they arrived at the picnic on July 23, Deborah said, people were certainly surprised but not upset. They embraced it and had fun. That was, Deborah is proud to say, "the last all male executive outing."[247] The next outing, held in August, was coed and was documented in a *Store Chat* photo spread with the headline "Boys and Girls Together at Executive Outing: Photos taken by R. B. Dallas, Executive Development Director, show outcome of change in plans for the annual executive outings. The August 27th outing at Haverford College drew 105 Associates, the largest attendance on record. A good time was had by all."[248]

Jennifer Gorman-Strawbridge

"I didn't feel like I was surrounded by men. Many of the people I worked with in the Advertising Department were women. We were led by a man. I really looked up to Natalie Weintraub and Thelma Aiken. My impression of women in leadership roles in the workforce was shaped by seeing them operate and by hearing my dad talk about them as leaders."[249]

DESEGREGATING THE DEPARTMENT STORE

Department stores offered the promise of democratizing consumption. Historian Traci Parker says in her book *Department Stores and the Black Freedom Movement,* "Stores operated under the principle of free entry and browsing."[250] She describes how all were welcome to peruse the stylish décor and merchandise, which stirred aspirations of social mobility and a middle-class lifestyle. The caveat, however, was that this new lifestyle was restricted to whites. Jim Crow laws of the South outright banned Black patrons from some department stores. In the North, "Black customers were welcome to spend their money on material goods in many stores but were frequently ignored and underserved."[251] Depending on the store, Black patrons might not be allowed to try on clothes or they might have to try them on at the back of the store, and some stores did not accept returns from Black customers. Traci Parker notes that S&C did not subject its Black customers to these discriminatory practices. It even advertised in Black newspapers. Some affluent Blacks went great distances to avoid discrimination. *Afro-American* publisher Carl Murphy traveled to Philadelphia to shop at S&C instead of department stores in his hometown of Baltimore.[252] However, it should not be assumed that Carl Murphy's relatively decent experience matched that of all Black S&C customers during this time. The level of integration at S&C was debatable. Historian Patricia Cooper found that although Black customers shopped at all the Philadelphia stores during the 1940s, "Stern's was generally considered to have the most integrated clientele, while Bonwit's, Wanamaker's, and Strawbridge's had the least."[253]

Regardless of how they might be treated, Black customers could rightfully assume that they would not be served by people who looked like them. Like most department stores during the first half of the twentieth century, S&C did not hire Black salespeople. "Stores hired them only as maintenance and stockroom workers, elevator operators, porters, and maids—all invisible from the salesroom floor"—and perhaps invisible to white employees.[254] Black employees who worked as elevator operators and porters were expected to wear a smile and be silent. They certainly couldn't react to customer or employee banter. In scholar Jerome Bjelopera's essay, "White Collars and Blackface: Race and Leisure among Clerical and Sales Workers in Early Twentieth-Century Philadelphia," he references an article from a 1909 *Store Chat* issue about proper employee conduct in the elevators. The article admonished saleswomen who use the elevator as a place to informally gather and gossip. Bjelopera surmises that to the white saleswomen, the Black operator was of little or no consequence and presented no threat to their ability to talk freely.[255]

All of which raises the uncomfortable question: Were Black employees and employees who did not identify as white fully accepted into the Store Family? There was clearly a level of appreciation for the roles they filled. Signs of that are seen in several *Store Chat* issues. A 1910 issue contains a death announcement for Charles G. Williams, a Black man who worked at the store for twenty-three years and was in charge of the basement lavatories. The announcement describes Charles, beloved by many, as "one of the most highly regarded members of our Store Family." S&C *Store Chat* issues from the 1950s show photos of annual employee breakfasts and luncheons held to thank the kitchen staff, cooks and housekeeping staff, who were nearly all Black. Yet research into *Store Chat* issues up until the late 1940s reveals very few photos of Black or non-white employees taking part in the larger company culture. Only white employees are seen participating in employee sports events and clubs, enjoying time at the beach in Wildwood, New Jersey, and attending the Quarter Century Club banquets.

Two Groups representative of the Fine Body of Colored Men composing our Force of
Elevator Operators

Elevator porters, 1912. *Courtesy of the Hagley Museum and Library.*

Good Housekeeping Group coffee and doughnuts, 1951. *Courtesy of the Hagley Museum and Library.*

Even a company that prided itself on promoting camaraderie and opportunity for all succumbed to and actively perpetuated racist biases of the time—some more blatant than others, including racist humor and stories in early issues of *Store Chat*. For example, a 1911 issue contains a racist parable that uses "so-called black characteristics such as laziness, drunkenness, and stupidity" to convey to readers the importance of hard work, abstinence and personal conduct.[256] There were the minstrel clubs, too, which Traci Parker says "pervaded American department store culture."[257] The Clover Mandolin Club was formed in 1906 by women, and the Argyle Minstrel Club was formed in 1912 by men.[258] Both performed frequently for special store events.

It wasn't until after World War II that S&C, along with many other department stores, began hiring Black salespeople. In Philadelphia, this change was largely due to the tireless efforts of the Committee on Fair Employment Practices in Department Stores (CEPDS), which formed under the direction of the American Friends Service Committee's (AFSC)

Jobs Program. It was a coalition of several organizations that included the AFSC, the Pennsylvania NAACP, the Women's International League, the American Jewish Congress and many others. Its mission was to address discriminatory employment practices of the time. Across the labor market, returning Black soldiers struggled with reclaiming their old jobs as employers gave preferential treatment to returning white soldiers. Black workers who stayed home during the war and worked in war agencies and production faced postwar layoffs and difficulty finding jobs elsewhere. Black women also lost their skilled wartime jobs and had to return to less secure domestic work.

One of several racist images in early issues of *Store Chat*, 1911. *Courtesy of the author.*

Department stores played their part in white preference. They, too, displaced Black workers with returning white soldiers and "white saleswomen who had left for higher-paying defense work during the war but were discharged thereafter."[259] The CEPDS wanted to use department stores as an example of overall racial discrimination in employment. Its hope was to generate public attention around the issue and encourage legislative changes. The CEPDS "worked to create positive publicity by quietly convincing store officials that the hiring of African American sales and clerical workers not only would be well received by their customers and staffs but also would be 'safe…[and] profitable.'"[260] Between 1945 and 1948, committee members met with the top executives of the city's major department stores, including S&C's Herbert Tily. However, Tily and S&C's vice president, Howard Cooper Johnson, were unmoved by the request and expressed fears that hiring Black workers in sales and other more visible positions would "alienate white customers."[261] Even S&C's founding Quaker values of fairness and equality (Johnson himself was a "birthright Friend") could not dismantle deep-rooted racial bias. It would not be until Philadelphia's city council passed a municipal Fair Employment Practices Commission ordinance in February 1948 that S&C and other department stores ended their discriminatory employment practices.[262] By April, S&C had hired its first Black salesperson.[263] Documentation of this hiring is not located in S&C's archival records. However, former director

Top: Dumont's Minstrels, 1910. *Bottom*: Mandolin Club Minstrels, 1910. *Courtesy of the author.*

of S&C's Food Hall Robert Cressy provided an anecdotal account of this historical decision.

One of Robert's first jobs at S&C was as a department manager in 1967 at the newly opened Plymouth Meeting branch store. He managed Tabletop, Lamps, Gifts, Pictures and Mirrors. Robert remembers one of his saleswomen was a transfer from Eighth and Market named Madelyn Madison. An older woman, she claimed to be the first Black person to be put in a sales position. She told Robert that when she first began working at S&C many years earlier, she was the maid in the Silver Department, keeping the merchandise polished and clean. Over the years, she was able to absorb information about the merchandise from the seasoned saleswomen around her. As her story goes, one day, a member of the Strawbridge family was shopping in the department and was assisted by a new sales associate who did not know the merchandise well. Madelyn stepped in to help. The customer was so impressed that they went to Personnel to demand that Madelyn be put in sales.

According to Robert, "I have nothing but word of mouth to verify this story but believe it could be true as Madelyn was an excellent salesperson."[264]

Some signs of greater employee integration are seen in a handful of photos in *Store Chat* issues from the 1950s and early 1960s. A few Black employees appear in chorus photos and at Quarter Century Club banquets. According to Leonard Shea, S&C "was not anxious at the time to hire numerous Black applicants."

In response to the assassination of Dr. Martin Luther King Jr., the company formally observed Dr. King's burial on April 9, 1968. At ten thirty that morning, the lights in the stores dimmed, and business ceased while employees and customers shared a moment of silence. TVs were placed around the stores for people to watch the funeral service. Employees who wished to attend religious services were allowed to leave work to do so. The Eighth and Market Store reserved one of its display windows for a memorial to Dr. King, and space was purchased in the newspaper to "express the sympathy of the Company and its Store Family."[*]

---

* *Store Chat* 60, no. 3 (April 1968): 3.

Although applications for Blacks were specifically marked, it served no real purpose, since the company had no quotas. When he was assigned to the Ardmore branch store's personnel office in 1963, Leonard remembers being encouraged to hire Black women and place them near the store entrances where they would be seen. He said that it wasn't until the Civil Rights Act of 1964 had passed that the company began to be more "enthusiastic" about hiring Black employees. Recruitment efforts were made through various programs like Job Corps, Youth Corps and the Opportunities Industrialization Center. S&C also recruited from predominately Black colleges in the region. Although top leadership supported these efforts, not all managers were on board with hiring Blacks at the time, creating obstacles for the Personnel Department. Older managers with long-standing prejudices resisted. Opposition also came from the unionized warehouse workers. According to Leonard, many were Italian and "feared their low skill jobs would be lost to Blacks who would be willing to work for lower wages."[265] It became harder for employers to discriminate after the 1971 Supreme Court decision in the civil rights case *Griggs v. Duke Power Company*. S&C, like many employers at the time, had to cease using intelligence tests in its hiring practices.

In 1972, Leonard moved to the Clover division, where he eventually became the VP for personnel and services and remained in that position until 1996. He recalls that resistance to integrating staff sometimes came from outside of the company. "Frankly, it depended upon the racial mixture in the very diverse area we served—from the Lehigh Valley to the New Jersey Shore to Delaware. The numbers of Black hourly payroll Associates varied from the very few in the Lehigh Valley and Frankford Avenue where there was neighborhood resistance, to 95% at Cheltenham Avenue to 40–50% at Rising Sun and the Gallery to 40% in the Central Office."[266]

The Supreme Court ruled in *Griggs v. Duke Power Company* that "even if there is no discriminatory intent, an employer may not use a job requirement that functionally excludes members of a certain race if it has no relation to measuring performance of job duties. Testing or measuring procedures cannot be determinative in employment decisions unless they have some connection to the job."*

Leonard still has a copy of a letter he received in the fall of 1978 from a disgruntled customer of the Feasterville Clover store in predominantly white Bucks County. The customer wrote, "Neighbors here are disappointed at your ratio of employment. This is a strictly white neighborhood and hiring 80% black is bound to bring up conflicts—these people will want to rent apartments or houses."

According to Francis R. Strawbridge, S&C and Clover passed formal antidiscrimination policies in the 1970s. Progress was slow, though. Sandra Jackson remembers very few Black Sales Associates at S&C when she worked as copy chief in the 1970s. In the Advertising Department, she was the only Black writer for ten years, and there was one Black art director. Still, Sandra said, "I think the advertising department was more culturally aware than other places I've worked since."[267]

* *Griggs v. Duke Power Co.*, 401 U.S. 424 (1971), Justia, https://supreme.justia.com/cases/federal/us/401/424/.

Although no employee demographic data for S&C could be found, Clover's Leonard Shea kept personal notes that document in 1996, there was one Clover store manager who was Black out of twenty-seven and one Black divisional manager out of twenty-one.

Like the country itself, the company was changing and responding to the political and social outcomes of the civil rights movement and other progressive movements of the early and mid-twentieth century. As seen with the progress of women, steps toward greater racial integration were also slowly occurring. Had the company survived into the twenty-first century, perhaps there would have been greater progress.

E. SPENCER QUILL

E. Spencer Quill. *Courtesy of E. Spencer Quill.*

The first and only non-white person to hold a corporate officer position at S&C was E. Spencer Quill, a third-generation Chinese American. He was elevated to vice president for administration and distribution in the Clover division in 1990, after starting at S&C in 1966 and later becoming one of the first Clover employees in 1970.

In many ways, Spencer was a perfect fit for the company. Like the founders, he had Quaker roots. He grew up in a Quaker community in Bucks County and received a Quaker education at the George School and Haverford College. Spencer also had a strong work ethic, which he attributes to his father. However, it took a long time before he felt like he belonged.

"I was probably very self-conscious about being Chinese," Spencer said. He remembers feeling this way for his first twenty years with the company. Growing up in a predominantly white community, he was targeted as a kid and has memories of being beaten up while walking home from school. Spencer carried his feelings of self-consciousness with him into the navy, where he spent three years as an officer. His captain even noted on one of his reports that he would make an excellent candidate for future promotions despite his obvious sensitivity about being "Oriental."

Once out of the navy, Spencer had no idea what to do, so he sought the help of a headhunter, who arranged for an interview at S&C. In December 1966, he started his first job with the company, stocking socks in the Men's Department at the Eighth and Market store. After one month, he became assistant manager in Accounts Receivable, where he supervised a staff of 180 women. New to the world of accounting, he was particularly grateful to the two women who supervised and trained him—especially when they took him aside and told him that he wasn't in the service anymore and needed to speak kindlier to the staff. "I took that to heart," he said. After eighteen months, he became associate manager.

When Clover emerged, Spencer was asked by his mentor and good friend Bill Rittmayer, who became VP and controller of Clover, to transfer to the new division. Spencer said, "That became the bulk of my career." Clover would also be where Spencer could put his natural aptitude for spatial relations to use. He was tasked with figuring out how to move merchandise around efficiently as it came into branch stores and minimize its handling before it went out onto the selling floor. He embraced the challenge and came up with creative new solutions, one of which included designing a new overhead conveyer system to take the place of rolling clothing racks, which took up too much space in the back rooms. Soon, every Clover store was retrofitted with the overhead system. Spencer recalls the many technological developments that occurred during those early years with Clover and how he was in a position to dive in and help.

"It was learn as you go, but it was almost like make it up as you go," he said. "That's what made my career so much fun. I was given license to come up with new ideas. That's what makes anyone's job enjoyable…the satisfaction of looking at something and saying, 'I did that.'"

It was this sense of accomplishment that finally boosted Spencer's self-confidence. "Once I got over my background, I realized I'm part of this family; I can do it, no matter what they throw at me. I think people recognized that."

Spencer's role in the Store Family would be cemented when he became Clover's VP for administration and distribution in 1990. He remembers that the announcement was made at an annual Clover meeting to thunderous applause. "I was taken aback by it," he said.

Spencer's Store Family ties continue today. He and Bill still talk regularly, and he follows the S&C and Clover Facebook pages. He jokes that "we went through good times and bad and we're still talking to each other."[268]

CHAPTER 11

THE END OF AN ERA

Stockton Strawbridge once described how keeping S&C family controlled was,
"An ever-present objective comparable to inhaling and exhaling."
—"Strawbridge & Clothier: Family Owned Beacon in a Turgid Retailing Sea,"
Associated Press, February 25, 1990

S&C had long evaded the need to accept a buyout, takeover or merger. Several propositions had been made over the years going back to 1905, and rumors of a sale seemed to surface on a regular basis. Still, it remained a family-owned and -managed operation. Unlike many of its competitors, it continued to occupy its original location at Eighth and Market, while also branching out across the Delaware Valley. In 1974, Stockton, chairman of the board at the time, reassured shareholders that recent rumors of a sale were just that: rumors. The company's one-hundred-plus years of uninterrupted family management and participation, he said, "engenders a sense of proprietorship that gives added meaning to our reputation for fair dealing and friendly service. It says that we are local people running a local business—that we have a stake in the community—that the community's interest and S&C's interests are identical."[269]

Despite this fervent commitment, outside forces and a changing world continued to pose a threat.

THE FAMILY IS NOT FOR SALE

Prior to the store's ultimate sale in 1996, the most serious threat it faced started to percolate in 1984. Ronald Baron, a large S&C shareholder, New York investment advisor and institutional broker, began to make infrequent but persistent inquiries to S&C officers about the company's board of directors, along with unsolicited suggestions on how to improve company earnings. While he was initially met with polite resistance from S&C treasurer and secretary Steven L. Strawbridge, communication would grow increasingly tense.

Ron Baron. *Courtesy of the author.*

At the same time, threats were surfacing from within the founding family. Robert E. Strawbridge III, great-grandson of Justus, expressed a desire to sell his shares of S&C stock. Although he had served on the board since 1969, Robert had never truly been interested in the family business. "I wanted to be a New Yorker and a banker," he told the *Philadelphia Inquirer* in 1996. It was no secret that Baron had set his sights on Robert's shares and that Robert could be persuaded to sell to him, even if it meant jeopardizing family control of the company. In a proactive move to prevent Baron from gaining even more S&C shares, the board purchased all 779,000 shares of common stock from the Robert E. Strawbridge family, which equated to a $40,350,000 deal. Robert subsequently resigned from the board, "thus, terminating a single-family representation covering sixty-three years,"[270] starting with Justus's third son, Robert E. Strawbridge, who served as a director from 1922 to 1947 and as chairman of the board from 1922 to 1955; followed by Robert Jr., who served as a director from 1947 to 1973; and ending with Robert III. The sale of the Robert E. Strawbridge family shares would reduce the Strawbridge family's overall stock holdings to just under 50 percent.

Meanwhile, Baron grew more aggressive over two years of back-and-forth with S&C officers. On April 21, 1986, he finally went to the press to reveal his true intentions to acquire the company. The *Philadelphia Inquirer* and the *Wall Street Journal* reported his offer to purchase for cash 4,160,000 shares of S&C common stock, which equated to two-thirds of the company's outstanding shares, at sixty dollars per share.[271] S&C quickly responded by writing to its shareholders that it would reject Baron's offer.

Mr. Baron's offer is an obvious attempt to put the Company "in play" in order to attract other bidders since he has neither the financing nor the expertise to run the company....We feel a special responsibility to our more than 12,000 employees who, with their families, depend upon the continuing growth and successful operation of our company under family ownership and management. In this regard we do not feel that it is in the best interest of you, our shareholder, our employees, suppliers, and the communities we serve to turn over our business to Mr. Baron or anyone else.

The board's executive committee, in consultation with a team of lawyers from the Philadelphia law firm Morgan Lewis & Bockius, went into battle mode and devised a defense strategy, proving that even Quakers can fight. They agreed to a plan that would retain at least 50 percent holding of S&C stock by family and friends, including company employees. These shareholders agreed not to sell their stock for at least six months. The company easily achieved this goal, and by May 1, 1986, all complying shareholders had signed a Form 13-D (a disclosure form required by the Securities and Exchange Commission). The board also agreed to a reclassification plan of the company's common stock to further defend the company against any hostile takeover. Common stock would now be divided into two series: Series A, with one vote per share, and Series B, with ten votes per share. Shareholders would vote on these proposed changes at the company's June annual shareholders meeting.

Not surprisingly, Baron filed suit in federal court to ban the annual shareholders meeting. Frank Veale described in his book *Family Business: Strawbridge and Clothier: The Triumphant Eighties* that Baron's suit "contains the usual allegations under the federal securities laws, but he also gives the knife an extra twist by adding a count under RICO (the Racketeer Influenced and Corrupt Organizations Act)." As much as this claim may have insulted the board, it became clear that the deck was stacked against Baron since he filed in a federal courthouse a block away from S&C's Eighth and Market store. As Frank Veale put it, "The fact that over the years many federal judges have been our good customers probably does us no harm."[272] After four days of hearings, the judge approved S&C's reclassification plan on July 21, 1986, putting an end to Baron's takeover bid. The founding family members, the S&C and Clover Associates, shareholders and S&C's loyal customers all

In May, the company issued a full-page public statement in the *Philadelphia Inquirer* asserting its intention to fight Baron's takeover bid.

The family is not for sale.

More than 12,000 employees. Over 3,000 shareholders. Third, fourth, and fifth generation Strawbridge & Clothier descendents. We are a family.

And we cannot be bought. Nor will we allow ourselves to be used for someone else's gain.

This is *our* store.

And we have been minding it successfully for the past 118 years. What's more, we have absolutely no intention of relinquishing that hard-earned privilege.

We shall do everything in our power to retain our independence and integrity, trademarks that have made Strawbridge & Clothier one of the most respected names in the retailing industry.

On April 21, Ronald Baron, a New York investor, made an unsolicited offer to buy Strawbridge & Clothier.

The management of Strawbridge & Clothier views this as a "hostile takeover attempt." The Board of Directors *has rejected this irresponsible offer.*

A group of shareholders has joined together and signed an agreement stating their commitment to not sell their stock for a period of six months. The Board also authorized the corporation to purchase shares of the company's common stock in the open market in an amount up to $30 million.

We firmly believe that our independence is our greatest asset. The driving force that allows us to prosper while others, run by outside managers with limited understanding of our community, often falter. Sometimes fail.

To all the members of our store family, to our entirely home grown management, most of whom have been with the store for more than a quarter century, our regrets for any anxious moments this attack may have caused. To our valued customers, rest assured that it will be business as usual at Strawbridge & Clothier and Clover stores. And, lastly, to any and all who might consider following in Mr. Baron's footsteps, we urge you to think again.

NO SALE. NO WAY. NOT TODAY. NOT TOMORROW.

"The Family Is Not for Sale" announcement in the *Philadelphia Inquirer. Courtesy of the author.*

shared a jubilant feeling of victory. However, a victory announcement in the press had to wait until January 14, 1987. The final settlement had to be worked out, ensuring that Baron would not attempt any more takeover bids either directly or indirectly for three years. Baron also had to swallow his pride and comply with the provision that he write a letter of apology to the board of directors for making racketeering claims.

With this ugly chapter in the rearview mirror, the remainder of the decade proved to be the most prosperous years in the company's history. The year 1989 saw record sales of $950,306,000 and earnings of $31,159,000.[273]

The Final Years

Ten years after S&C's battle with Baron, the company finally succumbed to market pressures. The warning signs appeared at the dawn of the new decade. S&C, along with Dillard's and Nordstrom, Inc., were the only three large independent department stores still standing in 1990. Out of the three, Dillard's and S&C were the only full-line department stores offering not just clothing, accessories and home goods but also electronics and appliances. The 1980s had seen a merger spree among retailers, with the conglomerate May Department Stores Company leading the way.[274] Even S&C's longtime rival Wanamaker's surrendered its independence in 1978 when it was sold to California-based Carter Hawley Hale Stores, Inc., and then, later, to Washington, D.C. retailer Woodward & Lothrop in 1986.[275] ("Woodies," as it was fondly referred to by its customers, was owned by real estate developer Alfred Taubman, who acquired it in 1984.)

The '80s also saw the undeniable dominance of Walmart. "Walmart leapt ahead of both Kmart and Sears to become the nation's largest retailer....By the end of 1990, it was operating 1,725 stores, including 25 Sam's Warehouse Clubs. The company expanded into seven new states that year, one of which was Pennsylvania."[276] It would make its entrée into the Delaware Valley in 1994. This meant unwelcome competition for the Clover division.

The year 1990 was pivotal, too, since it was the year that Stockton Strawbridge stepped down from his position as chairman of the board's executive committee and officially retired after fifty-five years of service with the company. He would remain on the board as an honorary, nonvoting member. Peter Strawbridge and Frank Strawbridge became cochairs of the executive committee. Unbeknownst to them, the two cousins would be the last to fill this leadership role for the family business.

At the same time, a fifth generation was entering the business with ambitions to follow in their predecessor's footsteps. Jennifer Gorman-Strawbridge began her career at S&C as direct mail manager, after working at Filene's Department Store in Boston, Massachusetts.

Three years later, in 1993, Steven L. Strawbridge Jr. joined the company after completing a year at Woodward & Lothrop in Washington, D.C. He started as manager of the Men's Department at the King of Prussia branch store before eventually moving to the Eighth and Market store and becoming an assistant buyer for Girls 7–16. Steven jokingly remarked that Girls was where he learned the most about retail because of his unfamiliarity with the merchandise and customer.

The year 1993 saw the continued growth of Walmart. Its fiscal earnings that year came to $2.3 billion, more than the next ten largest retailers in the United States combined.[277] For S&C, 1993 marked the fourth consecutive year of underperforming earnings, despite an increase in sales. In the book *Family Business: Strawbridge & Clothier: The Final Years*, Steven L. Strawbridge describes how there was a constant focus among company officers on reigning in expenses. Decisions were made to combine department store and Clover division functions, implement a new health care plan for employees that required them to cost share, reduce the company's annual corporate pledge to the United Way, not open any new S&C branch stores or Clover stores and provide cash incentives to Associates to boost sales and reduce expenses through a company-wide campaign called "To Be the Best." Despite such efforts, the end of fiscal year 1993 would be the first time since the 1960–61 recession that the company did not declare stock dividends to its shareholders, "nor would it ever again."[278]

In the annual "State of the Store" address, Peter, Francis and Warren White shared the hard facts and encouraged the Store Family to "recommit, rededicate, re-energize ourselves."[279] Francis reminded everyone in attendance that "the most important thing that sets S&C apart from our competition is that we are able to satisfy our customers better than our competition....The customer comes first. This is why we're in business."

The unwelcome trend would continue in 1994. Despite ending that fiscal year with record-breaking sales of over $1 billion and a 13 percent increase in net earnings, it was not enough to declare a stock dividend.[280] Earnings were still 36 percent below the record set in 1989. The company faced a harsh reality as it moved into 1995. Intense competition was coming not just from large national retailers like Walmart but also from local retailers. Wanamaker's, with its owner, Woodies, had gone bankrupt in 1994 and was now steeply cutting prices in a desperate effort to raise cash.

> *Retail experts agree that independent chains such as Strawbridge & Clothier stand little chance against the buying clout of merchant behemoths, such as Wal-Mart or May. Discount businesses, like Clover, have been particularly hard pressed as bankrupt rivals dropped prices to liquidate inventory.*[281]

Amazingly, the company had not had to endure any layoffs so far, but it was clear more changes were required to keep it afloat. Company officers were dogged by the question of what further expenses to cut without altering the "basic character of the business."

Acquiring Wanamaker's

A glimmer of hope for a more sustainable path surfaced in January 1995: an acquisition. Federated Department Stores, another conglomerate, was in the process of acquiring R.H. Macy & Co. and pitched the idea that S&C join forces with them. Federated was very interested in becoming a dominant retailer in Washington, D.C., which was home to several Macy's stores as well as one Woodward & Lothrop store (parent company to Wanamaker's), which was in financial straits. Federated would gladly take the Woodies in D.C. but had no need for the Wanamaker's stores in the Delaware Valley—hence, their desire to find a willing partner to take on these properties.

Who better than Wanamaker's longtime rival, S&C?

The benefits of pursuing this acquisition, as S&C saw it, were fourfold:

- From a competitive perspective, it would reduce the number of players in the Delaware Valley market from three to two: S&C and Macy's.
- Defensively, the acquisition would prevent the May Department Stores Company (Federated's biggest competitor) from swooping in and taking Wanamaker's.

- The company would expand its market presence into Harrisburg and the Lehigh Valley, without adding new retail space.
- It would increase sales by over $140 million while adding corporate overhead by only $11 million.[282]

And so the roller-coaster ride began. After several months of negotiating the terms and financing of such a large deal, S&C submitted its bid in partnership with Federated, Boscov's and Rubin Real Estate of $640 million to the bankruptcy court and the Federal Trade Commission in April 1995. The only other serious bidder was the May Department Stores Company in partnership with JCPenney. On June 21, it appeared S&C's bid had won, pending approval. "Euphoria!" is how Steven L. Strawbridge described the feeling among all who worked on preparing the offer. Plans were set in motion, a purchase agreement was signed with Woodies and the bid was made public. Six Wanamker's stores would become S&C stores. What would Justus and Isaac have thought!

Euphoria turned to grave concern, however, when a mere month later, news came that May and JCPenney had come back with a new bid, even larger than what they initially submitted in April. They had waited to announce their new offer until "just one day before the deadline for competing offers set by U.S. Bankruptcy Judge Stuart M. Bernstein."[283]

By August, S&C and its partners found themselves face-to-face with representatives from May and JCPenney in a New York City bankruptcy courtroom. After a long and tense day, reality sank in. S&C could go no farther. It had increased its bid as far as it was comfortable. May's offer of $726.9 million was just too high. The massive conglomerate would now add Wanamaker's and Woodies to its large collection of retail chains.

Steven L. Strawbridge writes in *Family Business: The Final Years*, "Instead of the volume and profit six additional stores would have brought us, we're getting a hulking new competitor with enormous buying and advertising power. By the end of the Wanamaker saga, our stock price will have dropped from $23.50 to $18.75."[284]

THE SALE

Unwelcome matters were on the agenda at S&C's next board meeting later that August. Peter Strawbridge didn't sugarcoat the situation when he confessed that the challenges facing the company over the next few years were huge. He regretfully acknowledged, "Qualities that set us apart in the past have lost their importance to the consumer."[285]

For the first time in the company's history, it had to give serious consideration to selling. Although the options of staying the course, developing a new business or attempting another acquisition or merger were discussed, it became clear that they would all pose greater risks of large-scale layoffs and poor shareholder earnings compared to a sale. The company's 1995's fiscal year would end with a 2.3 percent drop in sales and a loss in earnings. Yet again, cost-cutting avenues had to be found, some of which included freezing benefits earned under the Employees Retirement Benefit Plan and making changes to the 401(k) Retirement Savings Plan. These were bitter pills to swallow for a company that prided itself on offering attractive employee benefits. In November, the company issued a press release publicizing its intention to "explore strategic alternatives for the Company, including possible mergers, acquisitions or sales."[286]

The news came as sweet music to the May Company. In March 1996, fresh from its acquisition of Macy's and Woodies and hungry for more, the conglomerate formally informed S&C of its intention to submit a bid for S&C department stores, while Kimco Realty Corporation set its eyes on the Clover division.

On April 3, one day before S&C's board of directors met to consider May's offer, Francis, Peter, David and Steven Strawbridge, the four members of the fourth generation, privately convened. It was an opportunity to share what they truly believed to be the correct course of action. Steven recalled:

> *As gut wrenching and distasteful as it is, as much as it goes against everything we have worked for and believed in for all our working lives, none of us can recommend, in good conscience, "staying the course." Somberly, the four of us agree that if May's offer is deemed fair and equitable, we would each vote in favor of accepting the proposal.*[287]

And so, after a special meeting of the board of directors that lasted two days, a unanimous vote was cast on April 4 to accept May and Kimco's bids and dissolve the company. All thirteen S&C department stores would now fall under the umbrella of May and operate as part of Hecht's but with the name "Strawbridge's" to maintain local appeal. Even the former Wanamaker's stores that May had acquired in 1995 and converted to Hecht's would now display the name Strawbridge's. Twenty-four Clover stores would

Phils win, but lose Jefferies | **Flyers beat Rangers**
First baseman injures thumb, could miss two months. **Sports.** | Gain a three-point grip on first place. **Sports.**

The Philadelphia Inquirer

City | **Friday,** April 5, 1996 | 75 cents in some locations outside the metropolitan area **50 Cents**

Strawbridge Is Sold; Clover to Close

Philadelphia Inquirer headline announcing the sale of the company. *Courtesy of the author.*

be acquired and liquidated by Kimco, which would work with the Rubin Organization to re-tenant and redevelop the properties. Three remaining Clover stores would be sold to other developers and venture groups.

The news hit the press immediately. Front-page articles about the sale were in the *Philadelphia Inquirer* for the next two days, and the news continued to be covered in the local papers for several weeks. Along with differing opinions from market analysts about whether this was a good deal for shareholders, there were quotes from S&C and Clover Associates, those most affected by the sale. Although the majority of the company's nearly fifteen thousand employees were able to keep their jobs after the sale was finalized in July, four thousand Clover employees were at risk of losing their jobs under Kimco. Under May, one thousand S&C executives were at risk of losing their jobs, including buyers, divisional managers and some administrative staff. All rank-and-file S&C employees were able to keep their jobs.

Approximately ninety-seven unionized warehouse workers also faced losing their jobs because of the sale. According to a *Washington Post* article at the time, the May Company chose to shift work to a nonunion operation in Baltimore.[288] Upset with this prospect, a handful of warehouse workers held a sit-in at the S&C warehouse prior to the final shareholders meeting in July. The sit-in lasted for several days before Teamsters leaders ended it in an effort to negotiate with May Company officials.

Understandably, some employees did not hold back when interviewed. "We're being sold down the river," was what one Clover employee shared with the *Philadelphia Inquirer*.[289] Another Clover employee, Noelle Reuther, expressed her feelings in a letter to the editor, "It is evident that Messrs. Peter, Francis and Stockton Strawbridge do not care what happens to their loyal employees."[290]

One article in the *Inquirer* described television sets in the stores that were tuned to the news and lots of nervous chatter among salesclerks. After watching the news on a TV in the fifth-floor showroom at the Eighth and

Hecht's was founded in 1848 in Baltimore as a family enterprise and operated in the mid-Atlantic region of the United States. It was purchased by May in 1959.*

---

* John DeFerrari, "The Hecht Company: Last of DC's Department Stores," Streets of Washington: Stories and Images of Historic Washington, D.C., January 14, 2020, http://www.streetsofwashington.com/2020/01/the-hecht-company-last-of-dcs.html.

Market store, one employee tearfully said, "I'm sad. I've worked here a long time."

It was not lost on company officers that thousands of people's lives and those of their families would be gravely impacted by the sale. Perhaps no officer was more directly confronted with this reality than Clover division general manager Warren White.

"It was hard to face them. Their faces were white—there was nothing to say," he recalled. Although he loved every moment of his time with the company, he admits that closing Clover was devastating. He was the division's longest-serving employee, and for more than twenty years, he shared the dedication of many other employees in growing the business. "So, when Clover Associates discovered that Clover was not only being sold, but being eliminated from the marketplace, they were devastated," White said. "All their work was for [naught]."[291]

Since most company employees were not unionized and May was technically not responsible for providing severance packages, S&C would have to negotiate for them—even if this meant eating into dividends for shareholders, which it did. Jane M. Von Bergen of the *Philadelphia Inquirer* explained that "May's $600 million payment includes the assumption of about $390 million in debt, including severance....That left about $210 million for shareholders, or about $20 a share." This was down significantly from a high of $27.75 just six weeks before the sale was announced. The terms of the sale were for a tax-free stock swap (S&C stock for May stock) instead of a taxable cash-out to shareholders. Still, some shareholders were upset with the twenty-dollar figure, as were some analysts. Others, like New York retail consultant Howard Davidowitz, saw the writing on the wall for a regional department store like S&C. "For Strawbridge, it's a bailout. I think they had a risk of losing it all."[292]

Whatever the press, there was still much work at hand to try to complete the sale. For the next three months, the herculean task of sorting out severance packages for those who, sadly, lost their jobs fell on the shoulders of David Strawbridge and the Personnel Department. The company contracted with an outside firm to assist these employees with their résumés and other items that could help ease the transition into new jobs. Personnel also aided with issues for employees who were staying and would begin working under Hecht's management. Together, David and his team oversaw what must have been a tedious, exhausting and emotional process for all involved.

Perhaps one silver lining was that there were three whole months to address all that needed to be performed, including farewells. As Steven L. Strawbridge Jr. noted, "I remember a camaraderie once the initial shock was over. There were tons of parties because it was a long going away period."[293] There was time to get the most out of the final days, share last moments and exchange information for keeping in touch, all of which, hopefully, helped to ease some of the sadness many in the Store Family were feeling.

For a moment, the old Wanamaker's building on Thirteenth and Market would also be called Strawbridge's, making for two Strawbridge's on Market Street. By August 1997, the name had changed once more, to Lord & Taylor, which came under May's umbrella in 1986.

There was time, too, for *Store Chat* to put out its last issue in July 1996, which was dedicated to the "Associates of Strawbridge & Clothier" and filled with photographs of all who made up the Store Family over several decades. Editor Dorette Rota Jackson's farewell message fondly read:

> *As we take our final bow on the great stage of retail giants, we won't exit empty-handed. We, the Store Family Associates of Strawbridge & Clothier, take with us the soul of a Company that will never be replicated….But most of all, we take with us the memories of an era that have united us as one family. As our final days approach, let us leave—not in defeat—but victorious in the realization that we have made our mark in history.*[294]

The last page was devoted to Francis and Peter's farewell message, in which they reminded their fellow Associates, "Without you there would be no 'family.' You and your predecessors—our Strawbridge & Clothier and Clover Associates—have been our Store Family since the first day we opened shop. Your loyalty and professionalism is unsurpassed and has always set us apart from the rest."

THE LAST ANNUAL MEETING

Although the twelve board members had cast their votes, the more than 5,000 shareholders—450 of whom crowded into the auditorium at the Eighth and Market building—would not cast theirs until July 15, 1996.[295] The scene was tense. "Not since the time of the Baron takeover attempt ten years ago has the eighth-floor auditorium been so packed with people." There was even a spillover crowd watching via a video screen on another floor.[296]

Isaac H. "Quartie" Clothier IV. *Courtesy of the author.*

Chairman of the board Francis Strawbridge presided over the meeting and spent much of the time fielding challenging questions and statements from shareholders. At the end of the question-and-answer period, votes were cast and counted. The sale was finalized with 81 percent in favor.[297]

It was perhaps cathartic that such an emotionally charged meeting would close with an impromptu and heartfelt message by Quartie Clothier, Isaac's great-grandson, who, although he never worked for the company, sat on the board of directors.

> *Surely, it is a sad day. There has been so much pain; none of us wanted this. But it is also a day of thanksgiving. A day to thank all the employees who have made the great store what it is, and to wish them the brightest future. A day to thank our colleagues on the Board, particularly the four Strawbridges. It has been painful for them, too, so much more so because of the pain they feel for their Associates. I feel their pain, like a knife in the heart. But they have conducted themselves in the most extraordinary and splendid way. Their dedication and loyalty have held the store in greatness these last few years.[298]*

The next day, the company published a full-page ad in the *Philadelphia Inquirer* thanking its customers, the Store Family, the city where it originated and maintained its flagship store for 128 years and the entire Delaware Valley region that embraced its growth and expansion. All Strawbridge & Clothier stores would officially close their doors on July 18, 1996, to reopen later in their new form.

Marilyn DeSalvatore, who started her S&C career in 1956 and continued to work for the company off and on in a variety of positions until it closed in 1996, described her last day working in human resources: "It was so sad. People crying on the elevator. I was entering invoices into the computer and I kept typing away. And was finally told I might as well go home. I would have stayed on forever."[299]

Most Clover stores ceased operating on August 2, 1996. Some remained open longer while their lease obligations were worked out. The last operating Clover store, located in the Shore Mall, closed on December 26, 1997. Kohl's Department Stores made its entrée into the Delaware Valley at this time when it leased nine Clover stores from Kimco Realty.[300] Some former Clover employees were able to secure jobs with Kohl's or moved to other discount retailers such as Target and Walmart.

S&C graphic artist Roy Miller designed the farewell ad. He recalls that the design wasn't changed when he submitted it to his supervisors. "Oftentimes, what you submitted would get picked apart and changed." They basically ran it the way he designed it.*

---

* Roy Miller, in discussion with the author, May 2021.

The tedious task of tying up all legal, insurance and accounting-related loose ends was assigned to the Wind-Down Team, a group of 160 led by Tom Rittenhouse, Alex Jervis, Bob Molloy and Steven L. Strawbridge. Ron Avellino oversaw all real estate matters.

> *My Wind-Down Team responsibilities were a terrific learning experience. But it was constantly overshadowed by the deeply saddening experience of selling the company and overseeing the liquidation of Clover.… This was a somber time as heretofore we were all products of a vital, multifaceted and all-encompassing organization.*
> —*Alex Jervis*[301]

On July 18, 1997, the company was officially dissolved, one year after all S&C stores had closed. With signatures signed and dated, Philadelphia and the Delaware Valley would no longer have their own independent department store.

THE FIFTH GENERATION

Steven L. Strawbridge Jr.

Steven L. Strawbridge Jr. *Courtesy of Steven L. Strawbridge Jr.*

"When we were growing up, we weren't encouraged to work at the Store. There was never any pressure to work at S&C." Still, Steven L. Strawbridge Jr. couldn't deny that the family business was in his blood. After completing a year at Woodies as part of the Executive Training Program for founding family members, Steve realized this was what he wanted to do: he wanted to follow in his father's and grandfather's footsteps and build his career in the family business.

He admitted that he probably "caught the bug" in his childhood. His earliest memories of S&C were of visiting his dad when he was store manager of the Exton Mall S&C branch store. His father later moved to the Eighth and Market store, where he became VP, treasurer and secretary. Little Steve was quickly charmed by the grandness of that store. "I remember as kids we would get so excited to go in," he recalled. He has fond memories of visiting his grandfather in his large office, made all the more impressive to a child's eye by its dark wood trim, paintings of World War II planes and a world map that covered an entire wall. "The coolest thing for me was my grandfather...the pictures of planes in his office.... Just hearing him talk about the business...was pretty incredible." Steve remembers having lunch with his grandfather and father in the Pickwick Room of the Corinthian Dining Room, where they ate peanut butter and jelly sandwiches—not necessarily what you would think the head of a big company would eat. Steve admitted that his grandfather was one of his heroes. He was also always impressed with his grandad and dad's ability to remember the names of all the employees they would talk to when making their rounds through the store. "Just the respect you would see when they toured the store, the respect you would see both ways...that's something I've tried to take with me in my career."

Like many other S&C Associates, Steve quickly became comfortable in his new workplace. He made friends, joined the softball team and even met his wife. "The Christmas parties, the clubs, the sports teams, long-term employees. It's not because of the pay," he said. "People stayed because of the culture."

At that time, Steve said, he wasn't too concerned about the company's future. "That threat of getting gobbled up by something big was always there. But we were in a good spot, so it wasn't a strong concern. We seemed to be in better shape than the other stores."

Steve recalls that things changed very quickly when Wanamaker's went out of business. "It was a tough time. I give a lot of credit to my dad and that generation. It was extremely hard on them. I was staunchly dead set against selling the company. I wasn't on the board of directors and didn't know all the details. I remember having some one-on-one discussions with my dad where I said, 'We have to fight, fight, fight.' Ultimately it was the right decision. I'm proud of the fact that we didn't close any stores or lay people off before the sale."

Looking back, Steve said, "I cherish the years I got to work with my dad and grandfather."

Steve took many of the lessons he learned in his three short years at S&C into his current career as the chief administrative officer for the Pro Football Hall of Fame, especially that sense of mutual respect and camaraderie among employees. Fortunately, his position allows him to oversee retail, which he still loves. Although he is in Ohio, he finds it hard to escape his association with S&C. "Even being out here, people talk about S&C," he said. In fact, when he interviewed for his job thirteen years ago, the head of sponsorship came in and asked him to autograph something for him—a yellow S&C gift box.[302]

Jennifer Gorman-Strawbridge

"I didn't as much want to go into retail as that's where I landed." That's how Jennifer, Peter Strawbridge's second daughter, describes her entrée into the industry. Her interests were in art and design, which she was able to apply while working in advertising for Filene's in Boston after college. She enjoyed taking part in the creative process behind ad campaigns. She always knew that S&C was a possible career path, but she never felt pressure to work for the family business. Then, in 1990, her father told her about an opening for a direct mail manager at S&C. She applied, got the job and found herself back in Philadelphia at the Eighth and Market store.

Jennifer Gorman-Strawbridge. *Courtesy of Jennifer Gorman-Strawbridge.*

Before joining the company, Jennifer said, she always knew it had a reputation for its collegial employee culture. But she confided that "you always have a healthy skepticism about what people tell you because your last name is Strawbridge." As an associate, she found the reputation to be true and attributed much of it to the way the company officers conducted themselves. "They really had a deep, deep caring for one another. They did then and they still do," she said. They set the tone for the employee culture. Jennifer also observed how well her father, grandfather, uncle and cousins worked together. "There was no drama, drama was not a part of it."

When she started her job in 1990, Jennifer was aware that retailing was undergoing significant changes. She recalls that the Advertising Department felt the pressure to come up with more value propositions and to think more strategically about how to package content. At the same time, she didn't recall feeling worried that they would go out of business. She thought that they could compete—until the Wanamaker's bid fell through. By that time, she had been nominated to the board of directors along with Natalie Weintraub. She remembers having board meeting after board meeting. Discussions revolved around figuring out the best path for the company. "Our role as trustees was to make sure we were doing the right thing by way of the shareholders and we were doing the right thing by all of the Associates, the Store Family. Those were the things that were weighing so heavily on us."

What proved to be the most challenging time in the company's history happened to coincide with Jennifer's new role as a mother. One week after being nominated to the board of directors, she gave birth to her first son. In December 1995, a few months after losing the Wanamaker's bid to May, she gave birth to her second son. Although she was very much invested in figuring out the "right thing to do" for the Store Family as a board member, she admits that she was also "just trying to be a new mom and do my job at work." She appreciates how different the experience was for her father. "My dad was living it and breathing it. It was so much pressure." Even though they didn't talk much about work outside of the store, Jennifer did feel compelled to write her father a letter letting him know that she ultimately supported the decision to sell and that she understood what a difficult decision it was for him to make.

Jennifer appreciated how respectful her colleagues in the Advertising Department were in not questioning her too much about the possibility of a sale, understanding that as a board member, she couldn't talk about it with them. Still, she was fully aware of their anxiety.

During her final days with the company, Jennifer recalls wandering around the store, saying good-bye to people, and just how weird it all seemed.[303]

Isaac H. Clothier V

Isaac H. Clothier V. *Courtesy of Isaac H. Clothier V.*

Isaac H. Clothier V "Chip" did not grow up with the same sense of kinship to S&C as his fifth-generation Strawbridge counterparts. His grandfather passed away when Isaac was a young boy, and his father, Isaac H. Clothier IV, or "Quartie," opted to pursue a career in law rather than retail. Still, both Chip and Quartie held a deep respect for the company and its history. Quartie's fond childhood memories of visiting his father's office at the Eighth and Market store likely influenced his decision to accept an offer to join the company's board of directors in 1975. He proudly filled a fourteen-year Clothier vacancy on the board. He would bring not only his legal expertise but also his kind-hearted and genuine demeanor and sincere thoughtfulness for his fellow colleagues.

Chip, on the other hand, did decide to give retail a go and accepted a job with S&C in 1980. He completed the Executive Development Program and worked his way from assistant buyer to department manager to buyer. However, after only four years, he decided to set his sights on business school.

"I loved the store and the family." But unlike his ancestors before him, he did not inherit a love for retail. "I just was not a big fan of retailing. It was a very reactive business, and I'm more inclined to a proactive approach."

Still, Chip made many friends during his time and has several fond memories, including an Anniversary Sale Rally where he and Steven L. Strawbridge played Isaac and Justus. He recalled how the sense of family extended beyond the family itself. There were multiple generations among employees, mothers and daughters and fathers and sons all working together. It was a very unusual situation.

Chip attributes a lot of his success in later years with companies like Nabisco to the skills he learned while at S&C—not just the practical skills, such as allocating and displaying merchandise, but also managing responsibility. Since S&C had only twelve stores at that time, young buyers like himself were given the financial responsibility to spread their inventory among the stores. In his words, it was a "sophisticated situation," especially for a twenty-five-year-old. It was very different from today's retail conglomerates, which have hundreds of stores and a team of people to allocate and manage inventory.

Chip had moved on in his business career by the time S&C was contemplating a sale to the May Company; however, he was able to appreciate just how trying a time it was for his father as a board member and representative of the Clothier family.

When asked how he and his father felt about the fact that the Strawbridge name remained on the storefronts after the sale and not the Clothier name, Chip jokingly replied, "Well, now I know how Roebuck feels!" referring to the old Sears & Roebuck store. In all seriousness, though, Chip said, "There was truly, I believe a very strong friendship between Dad and all of the Strawbridges and a tremendous feeling of affection for all of them."[304]

Geoff and Chris Strawbridge

The store was ever present in the young lives of Chris and Geoff Strawbridge, the sons of David Strawbridge. Both have fond memories of visiting their father in his tenth-floor office, watching the Gimbels Thanksgiving Day Parade from a colleague's office that looked down onto Market Street and spending time with their uncle France and cousins Peter and Steve.

Like Steve Jr. and Wendy, they never felt an expectation from their father to work for the store. Still, both decided to give it a try at the King of Prussia branch store during summer breaks in high school and college in the mid- to late 1980s. Geoff recalled first working in shipping and receiving and then moving to the selling floor the following summer in Men's Sportswear. After college, he decided to pursue the Executive Training Program for founding family members and spent a year at Parisian Department Stores in Atlanta. Although he completed the program, he concluded that retail was not for him and instead pursued graduate studies at the University of St. Andrews in Scotland and, later, a career in online marketing. For Chris, it was just one summer at King of Prussia, also in Men's Sportswear, before he decided retail was not the path he wished to follow. His interests would lead him to philanthropy and nonprofit development. Never did the brothers recall sensing any disappointment from their father about their decisions. Both described their father as a man of few words. "He was humble and very Quaker," Geoff said. Extremely proud of his sons for their own accomplishments, David was likely happy that they experienced even a small taste of the family business.

"I distinctly recall Dad saying that from his vantage point (I presume he meant in HR) that I and people of my generation were likely to have four or five different jobs over our lifetime.… This was a very different expectation than what he experienced," said Chris.

Despite their short time at S&C, Chris and Geoff left with valuable skill sets that they took with them in their careers. "The thing about retail is it's very tactile, very tangible," said Geoff. His experience handling merchandise, taking it out of shipment boxes and learning how to creatively display and arrange it has helped him in online marketing. "That design skill is really important.…I understand how to photograph products for online, so people know how to experience the product and purchase it."

Top: Geoff Strawbridge. *Courtesy of Geoff Strawbridge.*

Bottom: Chris Strawbridge. *Courtesy of Chris Strawbridge.*

Geoff said that both S&C and Parisians emphasized the importance of relationship building in selling. "If you develop a relationship with a client, they might come back.…I know how to work with people over the long term."

When reflecting on what set S&C apart from other large department stores, Chris said, "It was a really remarkable institution.…It wasn't unique, but there were unique elements to it.…It's hard to even conceive of an organization of that scale and complexity today operating in that manner, maintaining that sense of community. Imagine Tesla having choirs and

Other members of the fifth generation also tried their hand at the family business but ultimately opted to pursue personal and career opportunities outside of retail. These include Justus's great-great-grandchildren Wendy Strawbridge Cozzi and Emily Harvey.

softball teams and going on trips together....Part of it was the times, and part of it was the family."

When asked about the sale of the store, Geoff remembered getting a call from his father while at graduate school informing him of the impending sale. He said at first, he wanted to "fix the company."

"I remember feeling upset, angry and sad but realized it wasn't really my place to change that."

Chris remembered his father saying at some point that there was a strong likelihood the store would "not be able to preserve itself." Despite this warning, as Chris recalls, there was no drama around the sale.

"I look back and can't believe I had such little sense of the magnitude of the change that was about to affect our family." At the same time, though, he understands that this lack of "drama" and ability to maintain composure was largely due to the influence of his family's Quaker roots—for better or for worse.[305]

CHAPTER 12

GONE BUT NOT FORGOTTEN

Strawbridge & Clothier will endure as long as we have memories to share.
—Francis R. Strawbridge III and Peter S. Strawbridge[306]

Between 1997 and 2005, Delaware Valley residents continued to shop at "Strawbridge's." Whether or not it felt like the same store was subjective. Some likely didn't notice a difference, while others clearly recognized that the store was not the same, not just because Isaac Clothier's name was missing from the nameplate but also because of the change in customer service and attention to detail.

S&C buyer Betsy Horen felt that the intimacy between salespeople and customers began to fade. She remembered how customers would call salespeople on the phone to ask about new merchandise or how, in the hosiery department, the saleswoman would take a pair of stockings out of the box and hold them over her hand to show the customer what the color was like: "the extra touches," as Betsy referred to them.[307]

Warren White from Clover visited a couple of former Clover stores, which had been converted to Kohl's. He spoke with some of his old employees but admits that they were difficult visits. "The Associates were glad to see me, but their messages were sad. Some employees found employment with Kohl's, Target and Walmart. Most of the Kohl's transplants soon left as conditions were very different than at Clover."[308]

Deborah Faragher remained in her position as store manager for Cherry Hill for approximately a year after the company sold to May. Ultimately, it was the difference in culture that made her leave for good. "I felt they didn't really care about the employee and their concern for the customer was nothing more than lip-service....It did not inspire loyalty."[309]

In the continuous dog-eat-dog world of market capitalism, another acquisition bared its teeth when Federated Department Stores bought the May Company in 2005 (in 2007, Federated changed its name to Macy's, Inc.). The rivalry between the two retail conglomerates was over. A year later, all the nameplates on many of the Strawbridge's stores would change to Macy's. Not so for the thirteen-story flagship store at Eighth and Market. For the first time since J.C. Strawbridge and Co. occupied the corner 144 years earlier, there would be no nameplate. Although the top seven floors of the grand limestone building had been sold to an office developer years earlier, the remaining floors became vacant. In 2012, the *Philadelphia Inquirer* moved its offices into the building, filling some of the space, while the ground floor remained ghostly empty. In 2014, the retail store Century 21 moved into the vacant space, only to close a few years later

Not until 2019 would public attention turn once again to the building (and the company). The City of Philadelphia formally recognized S&C's place in the region's history and installed a historical marker on the sidewalk in front of the building's main entrance. The installation was fondly celebrated on December 17, what would have been Stockton's 106th birthday. Several former S&C and Clover Associates turned out on the cold, wet winter day to read the words on the marker, reconnect with one another and step inside the front doors of the old building, filling the emptiness with memories, laughter and some tears.

One year later, in December 2020, GIANT Heirloom Market moved into the ground floor, revitalizing the space while also preserving many of its original attractions such as the elevators, Il Porcellino and the brass chandeliers.

> *Our Fashion District store is by far The GIANT Company's most iconic project because of its unique history. Shoppers will see how we have preserved and honored the beauty of this landmark and integrated it into our work to connect families for a better future. As a company whose own story began in the Commonwealth of Pennsylvania nearly 100 years ago as a family business, we're proud to celebrate the legacy of the Strawbridge family through our newest GIANT Heirloom Market.*
> *—Nicholas Bertram, former president, the GIANT Company*[310]

On this site, Eighth and Market Streets, a Strawbridge & Clothier store had been located since 1868. Between 1861 and 1868 this was the site of J.C. Strawbridge & Co. In 1868 Justus C. Strawbridge and Isaac H. Clothier, two Quaker gentlemen, became partners. For the next 128 years the Company grew as the City of Philadelphia grew, employing and serving generations of Philadelphia and Delaware Valley residents. Strawbridge & Clothier was the longest standing flagship department store in the country at one location until it was sold to the May Department Stores in 1996. It was the oldest department store in the country with continuous family involvement in the ownership and management of the Company.
—inscription on the Philadelphia historical marker at Eighth and Market Streets

The legacy of the Store Family continues to be celebrated decades after the sale. S&C and Clover Associates attend annual lunches and holiday celebrations. Virtual connections have been maintained on the "I Worked at S&C" and the "Clover Department Store Alumni" Facebook pages (with over six hundred and five hundred members, respectively). Many S&C Associates have posted photos of the GIANT Heirloom Market, happy to see new life in their old workspace. Francis, Peter and Steve meet with their fellow S&C officers once a month for lunch. According to Warren White, even though the Clover division had a shorter life than the department store division, bonds have remained strong among Associates. Many "remain very close friends today; some started other businesses and employed former Clover Associates. Some will visit me in Florida!"[311]

The memories live on.

CHAPTER 13

STOCKTON

I started in the Executive Development Program of Strawbridge & Clothier on June 14, 1965, Flag Day, right out of college. During my first week of employment I had an occasion to drive into work. I parked on the 4th level of our parking plaza and went into the elevator lobby and pressed the down button. As I was waiting for the elevator a green Volkswagen Beetle came up the ramp and parked next to me. An older gentleman hopped out and vigorously strode into the lobby. He nodded, said "Good morning" and followed up by saying, "Never ride somewhere that you can walk." With that he proceeded down the stairs. Later that day I discovered that the gentleman was G. Stockton Strawbridge, our chairman. I never forgot the lesson he taught me and never again used the up or down elevator in the parking plaza for the remainder of my 31-year career at the store.
—Alex Jervis, vice president for control and operations, Clover division of Strawbridge & Clothier; senior operating executive, S&C liquidating trust (Wind-Down Team), after sale of the business in 1996[312]

That about sums up the vivacious character of George Stockton Strawbridge. Why ride when you can walk? Why take the easy route when you can challenge yourself?

Not only was that how Stockton lived his life, it was also how he led the company, taking on one challenge after another as he strove to make S&C and Clover into the region's dominant department store and discount store—dominant not just in terms of the number of branch stores but in customer service and employee relations.

G. Stockton Strawbridge. *Courtesy of the author.*

A native Philadelphian with a long family history rooted in the region, Stockton's deep love for the area was reflected in his work, both with the company and with his civic engagement. Like his father and grandfather, he sat on the boards of various local nonprofit organizations, hospitals, schools and trade organizations. His crowning achievement, though, was his commitment to developing Market Street East. By the 1970s, Philadelphia's shopping district had grown dilapidated and uninviting. Stockton's vision was to turn it into the likes of the Champs-Élysées, cleaning it up and building what was, at the time, the nation's largest indoor shopping center, Gallery I, in 1977 and Gallery II in 1983. S&C, JCPenney and Gimbels would be the anchor department stores, with indoor entrances connecting them to the mall. Stockton was involved every step of the way, fundraising, meeting with city officials and partaking in the planning and construction process. He continued to fundraise and promote cleanup efforts of the city's retail center after his retirement from S&C. His tireless devotion to the project along with his numerous civic contributions were formally recognized in 1989 when he received the city's esteemed Philadelphia Award.

Understanding this background, one can see why it was so hard for Stockton to accept the board's decision to sell in 1996. For a man who, despite retiring, continued to be involved in the company as an honorary board member and routinely made the thirty-minute drive from his home to his office at Eighth and Market and chatted with employees during his regular rounds on the shopping floor, telling them he was still going strong even at eighty-three years old, it was clearly impossible to let go. The family business and the Store Family were his life. As his son Peter Strawbridge described in *Family Business: Strawbridge & Clothier: The Final Years*, Stockton viewed his work as a "sacred trust that he felt he had been given by the second generation."[313]

Sadly, Peter acknowledged that "the final years of the store coincided with the beginning of Dad's failing health." Dementia had taken hold of Stockton's mind. For the fourth and fifth generation of Strawbridges who had made the family business their career, trying to make their family patriarch understand how the company might suffer even greater losses and possibly become unrecognizable should it continue to forge ahead was excruciating and heartbreaking.

Reflecting on this period, Peter pondered, "If he had been able with a clear mind to look at S&C's future, might he have supported the Board's decision? On the other hand, in his case the man was the store and the store was the man. The two were inseparable. Had he supported the decision to sell the Company, not only would Dad have been breaking the trust, he would have been selling himself. Would his emotional attachment always have been so great that he could never have brought himself to sell? Regrettably, these are questions that will never be answered."[314]

Ultimately, Stockton's vision of continuing the company's growth well beyond the fourth and fifth generations did not come to fruition. What was realized, though, were integrity and character—the foundation stones laid by Justus and Isaac in 1868. The belief in and practice of these values has kept the spirit of the Store Family alive from S&C's beginning to its closing to now, twenty-six years later. A common refrain I heard from so many of the voices in this book, whether it was someone who worked a part-time summer job or someone who had a thirty-five-year career with the company, was how fortunate they felt to have had their time at S&C and

Clover, and how they carried what they learned into the jobs and careers that followed—whether that be stellar customer service, mutual respect or a strong sense of camaraderie.

S&C was not a perfect company. For every fond memory or word of praise, there is likely a fault or complaint. I have tried to address the ones I am aware of, but I am sure there are more. Nonetheless, the history presented in these pages, along with the personal stories and memories, depicts an older way of doing business that stands in stark contrast to many of today's business practices. Voices and experiences from the past inform the future. A job does not have to be just a job with no sense of growth or connection. A business does not have to meet bottom-line goals and serve shareholder interests at the expense of fostering positive employee relationships and community. Today's conglomerate retailers and online behemoths could learn a lot from a look into the past.

FINAL THOUGHTS

Mixing family with business is a risky endeavor. Love and trust can become victim to enormous stress and pressure. The family can crumble. Remarkably, that was not the case for either the Strawbridges or the Clothiers. The families managed to stay intact, and friendships between the two continue today. Perhaps this is attributable to the passed-down Quaker practices of quiet contemplation, discernment and mutual respect that might have aided each generation through difficult and tense times. Or perhaps it was just luck.

Left: Justus C. Strawbridge. *Courtesy of the Hagley Museum and Library.*

Right: Isaac H. Clothier. *Courtesy of the Hagley Museum and Library.*

POSTSCRIPT

S&C (the Store) was a very positive experience. I, and the three other family members of our generation, who spent our working lives there (my cousin Peter, my brother, Dave, and my cousin Steve), all felt the same way. It was a family-based Company that included the members of the founding families and all the Associates. We worked together wanting to stay independent for as long as we could. We had the same goals—our success and our independence.
—Francis R. Strawbridge III[315]

APPENDIX

Founding Family Members of Strawbridge & Clothier

A family tree of the founding family members. *Courtesy of the author.*

S&C DEPARTMENT STORES
AND CLOVER DIVISION STORES

Department Stores

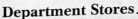

PHILADELPHIA—1868
8th and Market Streets
Philadelphia, PA

ARDMORE—1930
Lower Merion Township
Montgomery County, PA

CHERRY HILL MALL—1961
Cherry Hill Township
Camden County, NJ

SPRINGFIELD—1964
Springfield Township
Delaware County, PA

PLYMOUTH MEETING
MALL—1966
Montgomery County, PA

NESHAMINY MALL—1968
Bensalem Township
Bucks County, PA

ECHELON MALL—1970
Voorhees Township
Camden County, NJ

EXTON SQUARE—1973
West Whiteland Township
Chester County, PA

CHRISTIANA MALL—1978
Interstate Route 95
New Castle County, DE

BURLINGTON MALL—1982
Burlington Township
Burlington County, NJ

CONCORD MALL—1983
Brandywine Hundred
New Castle County, DE

THE COURT AT
KING OF PRUSSIA—1988
Upper Merion Township
Montgomery County, PA

WILLOW GROVE PARK—1988
Abington Township
Montgomery County, PA

CONCORD MALL
HOME FURNISHINGS—1995
Brandywine Hundred
New Castle County, DE

Clover Stores

MARLTON—1971
Cherry Hill Township
Camden County, NJ

BLACKWOOD—1971
Gloucester Township
Camden County, NJ

CINNAMINSON—1972
Cinnaminson Township
Burlington County, NJ

MORRISVILLE—1972
Falls Township
Bucks County, PA

CENTER SQUARE—1973
Whitpain Township
Montgomery County, PA

BALTIMORE PIKE—1973
Morton Borough
Delaware County, PA

WESTMONT PLAZA—1976
Haddon Township
Camden County, NJ

ANDORRA—1977
Roxborough Section
Philadelphia County, PA

FRANKFORD AVENUE—1978
Holmesburg Section
Philadelphia County, PA

COTTMAN AVENUE—1978
Bustleton South Section
Philadelphia County, PA

BUCKS MALL—1978
Lower Southhampton Township
Bucks County, PA

MERCERVILLE—1979
Hamilton Township
Mercer County, NJ

GRANITE RUN—1979
Middletown Township
Delaware County, PA

WARRINGTON—1981
Warrington Township
Bucks County, PA

CHELTENHAM—1981
Cheltenham Township
Montgomery County, PA

WHITEHALL—1982
Whitehall Township
Lehigh County, PA

PALMER PARK—1982
Palmer Township
Northampton County, PA

RISING SUN PLAZA—1983
Olney Section
Philadelphia County, PA

TOWNSHIP LINE—1984
Township Line and West Chester Pike
Delaware County, PA

PARK CITY MALL—1985
Old Harrisburg Pike at Rt 30
Lancaster, PA

PENROSE PLAZA—1986
Eastwick Section
Philadelphia County, PA

WHITELAND—1988
West Whiteland Township
Chester County, PA

SHORE MALL—1989
Egg Harbor Township
Atlantic County, NJ

KIRKWOOD PLAZA—1990
Kirkwood Highway
New Castle County, DE

RALPH'S CORNER—1991
Hatfield Township
Montgomery County, PA

BRANDYWINE—1995
Concord Pike
New Castle County, DE

GALLERY—1995
Gallery at Market East
Philadelphia, PA

S&C branch store and Clover store locations. *Courtesy of the author.*

CHANGES TO THE EIGHTH AND MARKET STREETS LOCATION

Different stages of the Eighth and Market Streets locations. *Courtesy of the author.*

EMPLOYEE GROWTH

An approximate number of employees throughout thirteen decades of S&C:

1868: 30
1878: 278
1880s: 2,000
1912: 5,000
1930s: 3,000
1944: 3–4,000
1968: 8,000
1996: 15,000 (includes S&C and Clover Division employees)

IMPORTANT S&C MOMENTS

1868—Justus C. Strawbridge and Isaac H. Clothier open Strawbridge & Clothier
1875 to 1898—Series of expansions of the building at Eighth and Market Streets
1906—First issue of *Store Chat*
1906—First Clover Day Sale
1910—Creation of the Noonday Club
1911—The Seal of Confidence is registered

1930—Creation of the Executive Development Program

1930—First branch store opens in Ardmore

1932—The grand opening of the new Eighth and Market Streets store

1948—Hiring of first Black sales staff

1971—Opening of first Clover division store in Marlton, New Jersey

1976—Natalie Weintraub is promoted to VP of general merchandise, becoming S&C's first woman VP

1982—The Food Hall opens at the Eighth and Market Streets store

1984—Nancy Longstreth and Margaret S. Clews become the first women board members to join the company's board of directors

1985—The Dickens Village opens at the Eighth and Market Streets store

1986—Ron Baron's takeover bid of S&C is defeated in federal court

1994—Jennifer Gorman-Strawbridge is the first member of the fifth generation of Strawbridges to join the board of directors

1996—All thirteen Strawbridge & Clothier stores are sold to the May Department Stores Company, twenty-four Clover stores are sold to Kimco Realty Corporation and three Clover stores are sold to other developers and venture groups

NOTES

Chapter 1

1. *Store Chat* 7, no. 7 (June 15, 1913): 156.
2. Alfred Lief, *Family Business: A Century in the Life and Times of Strawbridge & Clothier* (New York: McGraw-Hill, 1968), 8.
3. *Store Chat* 12, no. 7 (June 15, 1918): 102.
4. Ibid.
5. "Encylopedia.com," last modified May 14, 2001, https://www.encyclopedia.com/people/social-sciences-and-law/business-leaders/alexander-turney-stewart.
6. Lief, *Family Business*, 17.
7. Ibid., 17.
8. Stephen Nepa, "Market Street," The Encyclopedia of Greater Philadelphia, https://philadelphiaencyclopedia.org/essays/market-street/.
9. "John Wanamaker," PBS KCTS9, https://www.pbs.org/wgbh/theymadeamerica/whomade/wanamaker_hi.html.
10. Michael J. Lisicky, *Wanamaker's: Meet Me at the Eagle* (Charleston, SC: The History Press, 2010), 23.
11. Barbara McNutt (S&C stationery buyer), email to the author, January 28, 2023.
12. Lief, *Family Business*, 250.

Chapter 2

13. Rebecca, "Cash Register: The Complete History," History Computer, accessed June 10, 2022, https://history-computer.com/cash-register-complete-history/.

14. *Store Chat* 12, no. 7 (June 15, 1918): 101.

15. Lief, *Family Business*, 31.

16. *Three-Quarters of a Century: 1868–1943, Strawbridge & Clothier* (booklet published by S&C for its seventy-fifth anniversary), 11.

17. *Store Chat* 12, no. 7 (June 15, 1918): 103.

18. Lief, *Family Business*, 30.

19. Ibid., 30.

20. Ibid., 48.

21. Frank R. Veale, *Family Business: Strawbridge & Clothier: The Momentous Seventies* (Philadelphia: Board of Directors of Strawbridge & Clothier, 1981), 94.

22. *Store Chat* 59, no. 7 (October 1968): 15.

23. Vicki Howard, *From Main Street to Mall: The Rise and Fall of the American Department Store* (Philadelphia: University of Pennsylvania Press, 2015), 36.

24. *Store Chat* 12, no. 7 (June 15, 1918): 102.

25. *Store Chat* 12, no. 7 (June 15, 1918): 103.

26. *Store Chat* 59, no. 7 (October 1968): 16.

27. Howard, *Main Street to Mall*, 48.

28. *Store Chat* 12, no. 7 (June 15, 1918): 106.

29. Howard, *Main Street to Mall*, 48.

30. Lief, *Family Business*, 56.

31. Ibid., 57.

32. Ibid., 57.

33. Ibid., 89.

34. Ibid., 90.

35. Ibid., 104.

36. *Store Chat* 12, no. 7 (June 15, 1918): 103.

37. Ibid., 102.

38. Lief, *Family Business*, 104.

39. *Store Chat* 12, no. 7 (June 15, 1918): 102.

40. *Store Chat* 5, no. 9 (August 15, 1911): 1.

41. Marielle Segarra, "Were Retail Jobs Always Low Wage, with Few Benefits?," *Marketplace*, February 9, 2018, https://www.marketplace.org/2018/02/09/were-retail-jobs-always-low-wage-few-benefits/.

42. Lief, *Family Business*, 127.
43. Ibid.
44. *Three-Quarters of a Century*, 21.
45. *Store Chat* 35, no. 4 (April 1953): 3.
46. Lief, *Family Business*, 134.
47. Ibid.
48. *Store Chat* 6, no. 11 (October 15, 1912): 247.
49. Lief, *Family Business*, 150.
50. Ibid., 199.
51. Ibid., 128.
52. Ibid., 132.
53. *Store Chat* 85, no. 1 (January–February 1994): 2.
54. Ray Pascali, "The Big Store," raypascali.com, December 24, 2015, http://www.raypascali.com/Articles/TheBigStore.htm.
55. Ray Pascali, in discussion with the author, July 2020.
56. Clem Pascarella, in discussion with the author, March 2022.
57. Joseph W. Bongard, in discussion with the author, March 2022.

Chapter 3

58. Howard, *Main Street to Mall*, 53.
59. Lief, *Family Business*, 155
60. Ibid., 38.
61. Ibid., 40.
62. Ibid., 71.
63. Lief, *Family Business*, 236.
64. Alan Brinkley, "The Fifties," The Gilder Lehrman Institute of American History AP US History Study Guide, accessed August 22, 2022, https://ap.gilderlehrman.org/history-by-era/fifties/essays/fifties.
65. Lief, *Family Business*, 273.
66. Ibid., 272.
67. *Store Chat* 76, no. 2 (March–April 1985): 6.
68. Ibid.
69. *Store Chat* 56, no. 4 (June–July 1965): 17.
70. *Store Chat* 1, no. 1 (June 15, 1906): 3.
71. *Store Chat* 59, no. 2 (March 1968): 16.
72. *Store Chat* 1, no. 1 (June 15, 1906): 3.
73. Betsy Horen, in discussion with the author, June 2022.

74. Barbara McNutt, in discussion with the author, June 2022.
75. Paul Greenholt, in discussion with the author, May 2020.
76. Debbie Herron Jeffreys, in discussion with the author, March 2022.

Chapter 4

77. Francis R. Strawbridge III, in discussion with the author, November 2021.
78. Lief, *Family Business*, 175.
79. *Three Quarters of a Century*, 30.
80. *Store Chat* 24, no. 4 (January 1932): 4.
81. Lief, *Family Business*, 197.
82. *Store Chat* 24, no.4 (January 1932): 4
83. Lief, *Family Business*, 192.
84. Joseph Barrett, "Strawbridge's in Ardmore Is Turning 50," *Philadelphia Bulletin*, May 8, 1980.
85. Lief, *Family Business*, 191.
86. Veale, *Momentous Seventies*, 119.
87. Howard, *Main Street to Mall*, 132–33.
88. Ibid., 134.
89. Ibid., 134.
90. Lief, *Family Business*, 280.
91. Mike Monostra, "Throwback Thursday: A Peak into the History of the Cherry Hill Mall," *Sun Newspapers*, October 6, 2016, https://thesunpapers.com/2016/10/06/throwback-thursday-a-peek-into-the-history-of-the-cherry-hill-mall/.
92. *Store Chat* 84, no. 1 (January–February 1993): 5.
93. Jeff Gelles, "Strawbridge's Employees Bemoan a Family Tragedy," *Philadelphia Inquirer*, April 5, 1996.
94. Lief, *Family Business*, 295.
95. Ibid., 190.
96. Nancy Hemsing, in discussion with the author, March 2022.
97. *Store Chat* 56, no. 2 (March 1965): 6.
98. Lief, *Family Business*, 310.
99. Ibid., 249.
100. Veale, *Momentous Seventies*, 20.
101. Ibid., 35.
102. Warren White, in discission with the author, January 2022.
103. Veale, *Momentous Seventies*, 41.

104. Ibid., 135.
105. Ibid., 135.
106. White, discussion.
107. Pete O'Grady, in discission with the author, July 2021.
108. Steven L. Strawbridge, *Family Business: Strawbridge & Clothier: The Final Years* (Philadelphia: Board of Directors of Strawbridge & Clothier, 1998), 65.
109. White, discussion.

Chapter 5

110. Lief, *Family Business*, 102.
111. Ibid., 187.
112. Donna Elman Fine, in discussion with the author, May 2021.
113. Pat Foltz Martino, in discussion with the author, May 2020.
114. Ron Dipinto, in discussion with the author, October 2020.
115. Robert Cressy, in discussion with the author, June 2022.
116. Dan Rottenberg, "The Strawbridge Secret," *Philadelphia Magazine* 74, no. 1 (January 1983): 96.
117. Robert Cressy, in discussion with the author, June 2022.
118. Gina Major, in discussion with the author, April 2021.
119. Wesley Craig, in discussion with the author, July 2022.

Chapter 6

120. Lief, *Family Business*, 50.
121. Ibid., 52.
122. Ibid., 107.
123. *Store Chat* 59, no. 3 (April 1968): 12.
124. *Store Chat* 80, no. 3 (July–August, 1989): 7.
125. Lief, *Family Business*, 125.
126. *Store Chat* 59, no. 5 (July-August 1969): 15.
127. *Store Chat* 5, no. 11 (October 15, 1911): 246.
128. Lief, *Family Business*, 168.
129. Jeffreys, discussion.
130. *Store Chat* 31, no. 3 (March 1949): 4.
131. *Store Chat* 5, no. 12 (November 1911): 271.
132. *Store Chat* 53, no. 4 (April 1962): 7.

133. Susan Kearney, in discussion with the author, February 2022.

134. *Store Chat* 12, no. 7 (June 15, 1918): 104.

135. Fine, discussion.

136. Jeffreys, discussion.

137. Dorette Rota Jackson, in discussion with the author, June 2020.

138. Major, discussion.

139. Kearney, discussion.

140. Barbara McNutt, in discussion with the author, June 2022.

141. Miller, discussion.

142. Jackson, discussion.

143. Veale, *Momentous Seventies*, 170.

144. Ibid.

145. Pascali, discussion.

146. *Store Chat* 68, no. 5 (July 1977): 3.

147. *Fifty Years, 1878–1929* (pamphlet published for S&C's fiftieth anniversary dinner).

148. *Store Chat* 5, no. 7 (June 15, 1911): 159

149. *Store Chat* 80, no. 4 (September–October 1989): 10.

150. *Store Chat* 84, no. 1 (January–February 1993): 23.

151. *Store Chat* 77, no. 1 (January–February 1986): 8.

152. *Store Chat* 85, no. 1 (January–February 1994): 14.

153. *Store Chat* 40, no. 5 (June–July 1958): 7.

154. *Store Chat* 40, no. 6 (August–September 1958): 10.

155. *Store Chat* 33, no. 10 (November 1951): 11.

156. *Store Chat* 40, no. 5 (June–July 1958): 10.

157. *Store Chat* 79, no. 1 (January–February 1988): 8.

158. Lief, *Family Business*, 114.

159. White, discussion.

160. *Store Chat* 12, no. 7 (June 15, 1918): 101.

161. *Store Chat* 81, no. 3 (May–June 1990): 8.

162. *Store Chat* 86, no. 5 (November–December 1995): 9.

163. Frank R. Veale, *Family Business: Strawbridge & Clothier, The Triumphant Eighties* (Philadelphia: Board of Directors of Strawbridge & Clothier, 1991), 56.

164. Lief, *Family Business*, 112.

165. *Store Chat* 77, no. 3 (May–June 1986): 2.

166. D. Jackson, in discussion with the author, June 2020.

167. Jerome P. Bjelopera, "White Collars and Blackface: Race and Leisure among Clerical and Sales Workers in Early Twentieth Century

Philadelphia," *Pennsylvania Magazine of History and Biography* 126, no. 3 (July 2002), 471–90.

168. *Store Chat* 6, no. 12 (November 15, 1912): 287.

169. *Store Chat* 1, no. 7 (July 1907): 7.

170. Steven L. Strawbridge, email to the author, August 2021.

171. Jeffreys, discussion.

172. *Store Chat* 58, no. 1 (January–February 1967): 5.

173. *Store Chat* 58, no. 1 (January 1967): 5.

174. Pascarella, discussion.

175. Pascali, discussion.

176. Veale, *Momentous Seventies*, 154.

177. Roy Miller, in discussion with the author, May 2021.

178. Howard, *Main Street to Mall*, 50.

179. Veale, *Momentous Seventies*, 78.

180. Joe Nimerfroh, email to the author, September 2022.

181. Veale, *Momentous Seventies*, 94.

182. Ibid., 107.

183. Ibid., 107.

Chapter 7

184. Pascarella, discussion.

185. Kearney, discussion.

186. S. Jackson, discussion.

187. Rose (Shaw) Pontz, in discussion with the author, March 2022.

188. Bongard, discussion.

189. Major, discussion.

190. Susan Elfand Wiener, in discussion with the author, June 2022.

191. Marc Fox, email to the author, March 2022.

192. Veale, *Triumphant Eighties*, 104.

193. Ron Avellino, in discussion with the author, May 2022.

Chapter 8

194. Ellie Lord, "A Brief History of Holiday Shopping in America," *Lightspeed*, December 17, 2016, https://www.lightspeedhq.com/blog/brief-history-holiday-shopping-america/.

195. Lisicky, *Wanamaker's*, 83.

196. *Three-Quarters of a Century*, 23.
197. Veale, *Triumphant Eighties*, 82.
198. Ibid., 82.
199. Francis Strawbridge, email to the author, November 2021.
200. Jane M. Von Bergen, "A History of Fairness—and Fun," *Philadelphia Inquirer*, April 5, 1996.
201. Strawbridge, email.
202. *Store Chat* 6, no. 1 (December 15, 1911): 25.
203. *Store Chat* 52, no. 9 (December 1961): 2.
204. *Store Chat*, 81, no. 6 (November–December 1991): 2.
205. Pascali, discussion.
206. Michael Dailey, response to author's survey via Facebook, November 2021.
207. Susan Sander, response to author's survey via Facebook, November 2021.
208. Nancy O'Donnell Abbot, response to author's survey via Facebook, November 2021.
209. Michele O'Connell, response to author's survey via Facebook, November 2021.
210. Danielle Leon Speiser, email to the author, March 2022.
211. *Store Chat* 86, no. 5 (November–December 1995): 5.
212. G. Stockton Strawbridge, letter to Deborah Faragher, January 7, 1988.
213. Steven L. Strawbridge, email to the author, January 2023.
214. Betsy Horen, email to the author, January 2023.

Chapter 9

215. Dawn Downey Bundick, email to the author, September 2022.
216. Jim Hanley, in discussion with the author, June 2022.
217. Michael Drysdale, email to the author, March 2022.
218. Paul Greenholt, email to the author, March 2022.
219. Michele O'Connell, Facebook post, March 2022.
220. Ray Pascali, email to the author, March 2022.
221. Robert Phillips, email to the author, April 2022.
222. Francis R. Strawbridge III, email to the author, March 2022.

Chapter 10

223. Lief, *Family Business*, 140.
224. Ibid., 142.
225. *Store Chat* 56, no. 9 (December 1965): 7.
226. Lief, *Family Business*, 226.
227. Ibid., 231.
228. *Store Chat* 26, no. 11 (December 1944): 4.
229. *Store Chat* 56, no. 9 (December 1965): 7.
230. Veale, *Momentous Seventies*, 68.
231. Lief, *Family Business*, 193.
232. Ibid., 194.
233. Ibid., 198.
234. Howard, *Main Street to Mall*, 48.
235. Ibid., 49.
236. Howard, *From Main Street to Mall*, 49.
237. Jackie France, "Meet Me at the Fountain: Suffrage, Department Stores and Food," Digital Humanities Studio, Loyola University New Orleans, December 9, 2019, https://docstudio.org/2019/12/09/meet-me-at-the-fountain-suffrage-department-stores-and-food/.
238. Bjelopera, "White Collars and Blackface," 484.
239. Lief, *Family Business*, 151.
240. *Store Chat* 26, no. 5 (May 1944): 21.
241. Leonard Shea, letter to the author, September 2022.
242. Strawbridge, *Final Years*, 157.
243. Francis R. Strawbridge III, email to the author, February 2022.
244. Deborah Faragher, discussion with the author, February 2022.
245. S. Jackson, in discussion with the author, June 2021.
246. Natalie Weintraub, in discussion with the author, February 2022.
247. Faragher, discussion.
248. *Store Chat* 64, no. 7 (October 1973): 6.
249. Jennifer Gorman-Strawbridge, in discussion with the author, February 2022.
250. Traci Parker, *Department Stores and the Black Freedom Movement* (Chapel Hill: University of North Carolina Press, 2019), 16.
251. Ibid., 17.
252. Ibid., 51.
253. Patricia Cooper, "The Limits of Persuasion: Race Reformers and the Department Store Campaign in Philadelphia, 1945–1948," *Pennsylvania Magazine of History and Biography* 126, no. 1 (January 2002): 112.

254. Parker, *Department Stores*, 17.
255. Bjelopera, "White Collars and Blackface," 482–83.
256. Parker, *Department Stores*, 26.
257. Ibid., 25.
258. Bjelopera, "White Collars and Blackface," 486.
259. Parker, *Department Stores*, 116.
260. Ibid., 125.
261. Ibid., 128.
262. Ibid., 131.
263. Cooper, "Limits of Persuasion," 124.
264. Robert Cressy, email to the author, July 2022.
265. Shea, letter.
266. Ibid.
267. S. Jackson, in discussion with the author, June 2021.
268. E. Spencer Quill, in discussion with the author, June 2022.

Chapter 11

269. Veale, *Momentous Seventies*, 122.
270. Veale, *Triumphant Eighties*, 80.
271. Ibid., 93.
272. Ibid., 96.
273. *Strawbridge & Clothier Annual Report, 1989*, 8.
274. Strawbridge, *Final Years*, 19.
275. Jane M. Von Bergen, "The Grand, Beloved Old Strawbridge & Clothier Is About to Get a Historical Marker," *Philadelphia Inquirer*, December 15, 2019.
276. Strawbridge, *Final Years*, 25.
277. Ibid., 70.
278. Ibid., 71.
279. *Store Chat* 84, no. 3 (May–June 1993): 8.
280. Strawbridge, *Final Years*, 83.
281. Jane M. Von Bergen, "At Least 4,000 Jobs May Be Lost; May Co. Now Dominates in City," *Philadelphia Inquirer*, April 5, 1996.
282. Strawbridge, *Final Years*, 94.
283. Ibid., 98.
284. Ibid., 100.
285. Ibid., 100.

286. Ibid., 102.

287. Ibid., 116.

288. Frank Swoboda, "May Co. Plan Provokes Sit-In," *Washington Post*, July 18, 1996.

289. Jane M. Von Bergen, "S&C Sale Is One Chapter That Is Not Quite Closed," *Philadelphia Inquirer*, April 24, 1996

290. Ibid.

291. White, discussion.

292. Jan M. Von Bergen, "S&C Sale Is One Chapter That Is Not Quite Closed," *Philadelphia Inquirer*, Wednesday, April 24, 1996.

293. Steven L. Strawbridge Jr., in discussion with the author, January 2022.

294. *Store Chat* 87, Special Final Issue (July 1996), 2.

295. Jane M. Von Bergen, "Strawbridge Sale Is Up for a Vote Today," *Philadelphia Inquirer*, July 15, 1996.

296. Strawbridge, *Final Years*, 124.

297. Ibid., 124.

298. Ibid., 125.

299. Marilyn DeSalvatore, in discussion with the author, February 2022.

300. Susan Warner, "Kohl's Is Coming to Clover's Space," *Philadelphia Inquirer*, May 7, 1996.

301. Alex Jervis, email to the author, March 2022.

302. Steven L. Strawbridge Jr., in discussion with the author, January 2022.

303. Jennifer Gorman-Strawbridge, in discussion with the author, February 2022.

304. Isaac H. Clothier V, in discussion with the author, February 2022.

305. Geoff Strawbridge, in discussion with the author, July 2022; Chris Strawbridge, in discussion with the author, July 2022.

Chapter 12

306. *Store Chat* 87, Special Final Issue (July 1996): 13.

307. Horen, discussion.

308. Warren White, email to the author, February 2022.

309. Faragher, discussion.

310. Nicholas Bertram, LinkedIn message to the author, March 2021.

311. White, discussion.

Chapter 13

312. Alex Jervis, email to the author, August 2022.

313. Strawbridge, *Final Years*, 151.

314. Ibid.

315. Francis R. Strawbridge III, email to the author, September 2022.

BIBLIOGRAPHY OF IMAGES

The GIANT Company, Carlisle, Pennsylvania, 17013.

Mike Dougherty, reporter, KYW Newsradio 1060AM/103.9FM, an Audacy Station.

Personal collection of Betsy Horen, S&C buyer for Handbags and Small Leather Goods, 1970–96.

Personal collection of Nancy O'Donnell Abbot, Communications Coordinator for S&C, 1983–87.

Personal collection of Roy Miller, graphic designer and illustrator in S&C's Advertising Department, 1968–96.

Personal collection of the author, Margaret Strawbridge Butterworth.

Strawbridge & Clothier photographs and audiovisual materials (Accession 1995.250), Hagley Museum & Library, Wilmington, Delaware, 19807.

ABOUT THE AUTHOR

Margaret Strawbridge Butterworth grew up in the Philadelphia suburb of Merion. She moved to Scattle, Washington, in 1997 and currently resides there with her husband and two children. Margaret is a freelance writer for several Seattle-based publications. She has fond memories of shopping at the Ardmore and King of Prussia Strawbridge & Clothier branch stores with her friends as a teenager. For a special outing, she would go to the Eighth and Market Streets store, enjoy ice cream and chocolate croissants at the Food Hall, throw a penny in the Il Porcellino fountain and, occasionally, pay a surprise visit to her father, Francis, in his "Mahogany Row" office on the tenth floor.